Studies in Early French Taxation

By JOSEPH R. STRAYER

AND

CHARLES H. TAYLOR

GREENWOOD PRESS, PUBLISHERS
WESTPORT, CONNECTICUT

The Library of Congress has catalogued this publication as follows:

Library of Congress Cataloging in Publication Data

Strayer, Joseph Reese, 1904-
Studies in early French taxation.

Original ed. issued as vol. 12 of Harvard historical monographs series.
Includes bibliographical references.
1. Taxation--France--History. I. Taylor, Charles Holt, 1899- II. Title. III. Series: Harvard historical monographs, 12.
HJ2646.S75 1972 336.2'00944 78-138187
ISBN 0-8371-5644-0

Originally published in 1939
by Harvard University Press, Cambridge

Reprinted with the permission
of Harvard University Press

First Greenwood Reprinting 1972

Library of Congress Catalogue Card Number 78-138187

ISBN 0-8371-5644-0

Printed in the United States of America

To

CHARLES HOWARD McILWAIN

PREFACE

THESE studies were prepared independently and without the slightest idea of joint publication. When we exchanged manuscripts for benefit of friendly criticism we discovered that our results had a very real relation to each other, and this suggested publishing the two papers together. As our title indicates, we have dealt with only a few aspects of the early history of royal taxation in France. A great deal remains to be done in this field, and no discussion can be complete until M. Jusselin publishes the results of his extensive research. Meanwhile we hope that these studies may be of some use to scholars who are interested in the problem.

Both papers are primarily concerned with the means by which the royal government secured consent to or acquiescence in taxation. They differ, not only in their chronological limits, but also in their lines of approach. "Consent to Taxation under Philip the Fair" describes the numerous negotiations with individuals, local assemblies, and ecclesiastical councils in which that ruler engaged in his efforts to get subsidies. "Assemblies of French Towns and War Subsidy, 1318–1319" is focused on the relation of royal taxation to the use of large assemblies of towns in the period from 1314 to 1320.

Each of us agrees in substance with the main conclusion of the other, but each assumes independent responsibility for his own work.

J. R. STRAYER
C. H. TAYLOR

CONTENTS

ABBREVIATIONS

A.N. ....Archives Nationales, Paris.

B.N. ....Bibliothèque Nationale, Paris.

H.F. ....*Recueil des historiens des Gaules et de la France.* Paris, 1738– .

H.L. ....C. Devic and J. Vaissete, *Histoire générale de Languedoc,* new edition by A. Molinier. Toulouse, 1885.

Mignon ......R. Mignon, *Inventaire des anciens comptes royaux,* ed. C. V. Langlois, Paris, 1889.

Olim ....*Les Olim ou registres des arrêts,* ed. A. Beugnot (*Collection de documents inédits*). Paris, 1839–1848.

Ord. ....*Ordonnances des roys de France de la troisième race,* ed. E. de Laurière and others. Paris, 1723–1847.

CONSENT TO TAXATION UNDER PHILIP THE FAIR

BY

JOSEPH R. STRAYER
ASSISTANT PROFESSOR OF HISTORY
IN PRINCETON UNIVERSITY

CONSENT TO TAXATION UNDER PHILIP THE FAIR [1]

THE MIDDLE decades of the 13th century were a comparatively peaceful period for Western Europe. Rulers were able to concentrate on internal problems; they improved the organization of their governments; they defined, and in most cases, extended their powers over their barons. But this concentration on internal reform eventually led to a new period of war. The feudal age had left a heritage of overlapping rights and jurisdictions. Neither territorial nor legal boundaries were clearly defined. Yet the work of internal reform and consolidation could not go on unless these boundaries were defined. Unfortunately the definitions always seemed unfair to everyone except the ruler who made them. As a result, after 1280 every Western European state fought with one or more of its neighbors and quarreled with the papacy.

These new wars, largely waged to complete the consolidation of political units, show how far consolidation had already gone. Rulers were more powerful and they had more resources, so armies became larger and campaigns longer. As usual governments took chances in war they would never dare take in times of peace. They hired more men. Their budgets became permanently

[1] Princeton University, by a grant of the Shreve Fellowship, and the Social Science Research Council, by a grant-in-aid, made possible much of the research on which this essay is based. I desire to express my thanks to each of these institutions.

unbalanced. Yet borrowing on a large scale to meet war expenses was still impossible. So they were forced to do the thing which was hardest for medieval governments — they had to tax.

Taxation was unpopular everywhere at the end of the thirteenth century. In most countries large concessions had to be made to get the consent of those who paid taxes. By the second decade of the fourteenth century these concessions had frequently led to permanent limitations on the powers of the governments which granted them. Yet in France, where the need for money was great, where taxation was frequent, where opposition to taxation ran high, the government[2] seems to have lost little of its power. It seems to me that this problem is worth careful consideration. How did the French government get consent to taxation during the reign of Philip the Fair? What concessions did it have to make to get this consent? Why did these concessions fail to lead to permanent limitations on the power of the government?

France, more than any other Western country, was forced to war in order to complete her internal consolidation. The long peace of St. Louis' reign was shaken as soon as Philip III inherited the county of Toulouse.

[2] I hope some day to be able to discuss the question as to how far Philip the Fair personally directed the policy of his ministers. For the purpose of this essay it is unnecessary to distinguish between the decisions of the king and those of his ministers. As far as possible I have ascribed all acts to the "government," which the reader may interpret according to his own convictions as meaning either the king or his officials. In spite of this attempt to be neutral my own beliefs may have crept into the text and I should warn the reader that I feel, at present, that Philip had little control over his ministers and that many important acts represent the desires of the bureaucracy rather than those of the king.

This new advance of the French king in the South aroused the great feudal lords of the Pyrenees and the kings of Spain. The three wars of Foix, Navarre, and Aragon followed. And these three wars, difficult and expensive as they were, came nowhere near ending the opposition to the unification of France. In the four corners of the country were vassals with claims to independence. Two of them, the king of England in southwestern Aquitaine, and the count of Flanders in the northeast, had almost made those claims good. Attempts to enforce the authority of the central government over them would almost certainly lead to war. Yet if France were to be united the attempt had to be made. In addition all along the eastern frontier were petty feudal states, technically subject to the dying Empire, but actually closely connected with France by cultural and economic ties. It was almost impossible to define the eastern frontier without annexing some of these states, but such annexations were usually followed by rebellions of the local nobility. Philip III had defined only a small part of the boundary of the kingdom of France, and it is not surprising that his son was frequently at war.

The first years of the reign of Philip the Fair were peaceful. Perhaps the fact that the disastrous expedition against Aragon under Philip III [3] still had to be

[3] *H.F.*, XXI, 516, a statement, probably incomplete, of the expense of the Aragon expedition gives a total of 1,228,751 *livres tournois*. This is almost three times the king's normal income. *Cf.* tables in Borrelli de Serres, *Recherches sur divers services publics* (Paris, 1895–1909), II, Appendix A, where the income for 1287 (1294 for the *sénéchaussées*) adds up to about 430,000 l.t. This figure is perhaps a little low, since there were many local expenses in the *sénéchaussées* in 1294 for the war in Gascony. This money

paid for [4] had something to do with the reluctance to engage in new adventures. But in 1293 bickering with the English over Aquitaine led to war and the temporary conquest of the duchy. Before the French army of occupation had left Aquitaine, an attempt to bring the count of Flanders under the control of the French courts caused a new war in the northwest. A long and expensive contest ended with the partial submission of the Flemings in 1305. Eight years of peace, broken only by an expedition against Lyons, ended in a new dispute with the count of Flanders in 1313. The army was convoked that year, and again in 1314. While there was no fighting on either occasion mere preparation for war was expensive by this time.

Philip's real misfortune was that he had to fight two of the wealthiest rulers of the west. England was poorer than France but the English government was more powerful than the French and could obtain a larger proportion of the wealth of the country. Flanders was richer in proportion to area and population than either France or England. Now that armies, supplies, and even alliances had to be bought with money, waging war

---

would ordinarily have gone to Paris. An estimate of normal income from the *sénéchaussées* in 1313 was 20,000 l.t. higher than the figure given by Borrelli for 1294. On the other hand 1287 was a more profitable year for the king in North France than 1294, so the net ordinary income in the first part of the reign may never have been much more than 430,000 l.t.

[4] A.N., J 317, no. 49. A collector of the tenth granted the king for the Aragon expedition had advanced money against receipts from the tenth. He is allowed 54,199 l.t. for this in his account of St. John's 1286. B.N., ms. fr. 20683 fols. 3–5; loans totaling 60,800 l.t. were repaid in the accounting period ending Candlemas 1288; *H.L.*, IX, 175, another loan was repaid only in 1294; Mignon, no. 1103, some loans for this expedition remained unpaid as late as 1325.

was primarily a matter of finance. As Langlois says, the war between Edward I and Philip IV was a war between the pound sterling and the pound of Tours.[5] Both England and Flanders could afford to raise large armies and keep them in the field year after year. To meet such opposition the French government had to go far beyond its normal income. The dominant feature of Philip's reign is the financial embarrassment of the government. It could never plan ahead, it was always in debt, it lived by expedients. Although it invented very little that was new, it extended the use of money-making devices which had been employed under St. Louis and Philip III. Taxation became common and every tax was generalized. There was hardly a year between 1285 and 1314 in which some tax was not being collected.[5a] There was hardly a person in France who did not pay a tax at some time during the reign of Philip the Fair.

The taxes levied during Philip's reign fall into six main groups. First, and most important, are the taxes on the Church. The most common levy on the Church was the tenth, which was supposed to yield ten per cent of the income from ecclesiastical benefices. In practice, assessments became fixed at a low figure, exemptions were granted and the actual rate was lower.[6] Annates, that is, a year's income, less expenses, from clerics appointed or promoted to new offices, were also granted the king on two occasions. In twenty-four of the thirty

[5] Lavisse, *Histoire de France*, III, pt. 2, p. 297.

[5a] See Appendix I.

[6] A.N., J 1035, no. 36. See estimates of value of a tenth in *H.F.*, XXI, 541 and 560, where it will be seen that each province is assessed at about the same amount in 1294 and 1313.

years between 1285 and 1314 the Church paid either tenths or annates or both.[7] No other subjects of the king were taxed so frequently. No tax except the subsidies for war yielded so much money and the subsidies were paid by a much larger number of people. If there were not too much opposition nor too many exemptions, an ordinary tenth yielded about 260,000 l.t.[8] It may be argued, of course, that these impositions on the Church were not taxes of the French government since they were granted by a foreign authority and devoted, at least in theory, to religious purposes. This had been true under St. Louis and Philip III, but under Philip the Fair several tenths were imposed on the Church by the king without papal consent. Most of the tenths received by the government were used for secular purposes, especially for the defense of the realm.[9] Fortunately, for our purposes, the tenths in which the element of consent is most prominent were the ones over which the pope had no control. As for the annates, while they were always granted by the pope, they were used for purely secular expenses.[10] The government had less control over them than it had over tenths, and since the question of consent to annates never arose they will be ignored in later discussions.

The second group of taxes are the personal property

[7] Mignon, pp. 9–10; Borrelli de Serres, II, 462–468. See Appendix I.

[8] Borrelli de Serres, II, 465 ff.; *H.F.*, XXI, 545, 560.

[9] *Ord.*, I, 382; *Coll. de documents inédits sur l'hist. de France, Mélanges historiques*, II, 320; A.N., J 1035, nos. 36, 37, 38, 39, 40; all state that tenths are being granted for defense of realm. A.N., J 350, nos. 5, 6, show royal officials imposing and collecting a tenth by force in the province of Tours in 1305.

[10] Mignon, no. 535.

and income taxes paid by most laymen, and churchmen who had secular property, to finance Philip's wars. The form of these taxes varied according to the status of those paying and also according to the place where they lived, since each province and often each town made its own arrangements with the central power. However, three main types may be distinguished.[11] During the first period of the wars (1295–1300) the tax was based on the principle that all inhabitants of France, and not merely the military tenants of the king, were bound to aid in defending the realm. This principle was rather new, and was by no means universally accepted. Moreover, as it had been interpreted up to 1295, it meant only that all subjects were liable to military service. The government translated it into a right to take a certain percentage of everyone's property, without even going through the form of stating that these sums were taken in lieu of the service which all men owed. An attempt was made to minimize the shock caused by the innovation by securing the consent of the royal council, but this consent, while it might have justified a purely feudal aid, was not enough to justify a national tax. Growing discontent forced the government to shift its ground and from 1302 through 1304 taxation was based expressly on the principle of commutation of military service. All men were summoned to the army, and then were asked to pay certain sums for exemption. The wealthier people paid varying percentages, according to their status, of their income and personal property. All others, except the very poor, were grouped in arbi-

[11] Detailed references regarding these taxes will be found below, pp. 43–88.

trary units of 100 hearths, which paid lump sums for the wages of soldiers. There was resistance to this tax also, and this resistance may have helped bring about the rather unsatisfactory peace with Flanders in 1305. Between 1305 and 1313 the government tried to avoid general taxation. This was possible because there were no extensive military operations during those years. Moreover the confiscation of the property of the Jews in 1300 and that of the Templars in 1307 [12] gave the government important additional, if temporary, revenues.[13] As a result, during the period 1305–1313 only two general taxes were taken from laymen. They form the third type and are based on the unassailable principle of the feudal aid which is due as a matter of course. The aid for marrying the king's eldest daughter was asked in 1308, that for knighting his eldest son in 1313. There could be no legal objection to these aids, although

[12] H. C. Lea, *History of the Inquisition*, III, 229–230; M. Felibien, *Histoire de la ville de Paris* (Paris, 1725), III, 320–321. While the king turned over the property of the Temple to the Hospital in 1317, it was agreed that the revenues of Temple property between 1307 and 1317 were to remain with the king. The moveable property of the Temple was kept by the king to satisfy debts which he claimed the Temple had owed him.

[13] It has been said that the confiscation of Jewish property gave disappointingly small returns, e.g., Langlois in Lavisse, *Hist. de France*, III, pt. 2, p. 225. It is probably true that the court had exaggerated ideas about the wealth of the Jews, and that much was embezzled or concealed. Nevertheless it is clear that large sums were obtained and that income from sales of Jewish property continued for several years. S. Luce, "Catalogue des documents du trésor des chartes relatifs aux juifs," *Revue des études juives*, II (1881), *pièces justificatives*, nos. 34, 66, 92, shows that at least 87, 193 l.t. had been received from Jewish property in Toulouse by 13 Nov. 1310. Mignon, nos. 2151–2153, at least 104,430 l.t. had been collected by receivers of Jewish goods in Champagne by 1310. These are larger sums than either region provided for subsidies. B.N., ms. fr. 25,993, nos. 189, 194, 198; sales of Jewish property in Toulouse as late as 1312–14 yielded 1464 l.t.

some difficulty arose when the government tried to generalize them by taking them directly from rear-vassals and from chartered towns.[14] Unfortunately they could be taken only once and the Flemish war scare of 1313–1314 forced the government to revert to the second type of tax, that based on commutation of military service. Ten years' respite had not been long enough to dull the opposition to this tax and as a result of new protests the impost of 1314 was never fully collected.[15]

A third general group of taxes was based on sales and other contracts. Buyer and seller each paid a certain percentage of the sales-price to the king, often at the rate of a penny in the pound. The Lombards agreed in 1295 to pay such a tax on transactions among themselves in France.[16] This tax continued to the end of the reign [17] but seems to have yielded only twelve to thirteen thousand *livres tournois* a year.[18] Some towns in

[14] See below, pp. 77–81.

[15] *Ord.*, I, 580; *H.F.*, XXI, 570.

[16] Borrelli de Serres, II, 458; *Ord.*, XI, 377.

[17] Borrelli de Serres seems to be wrong when he says the tax ceased at the death of Biche and Mouche. A.N., JJ 45, no. 181, it was still being collected in 1310. *Olim*, II, 607, Parlement decides in 1314 that payment of this tax frees the Lombards from paying the aids for Isabelle's marriage (1308) and for Louis' knighting (1313).

[18] Borrelli de Serres, II, 458, the tax was farmed in 1317 for 13,750 l.t. a year. A.N., JJ 45, no. 181, Enguerran de Marigny bought the share (1/21) of Biche and Mouche from their heir and sold it to the king in 1310 for a rent of 600 l.t. Since Enguerran never cheated himself in his dealings with Philip IV we can be sure that the total annual income from the tax c. 1310 was not much more than 12,600 l.t. Borrelli de Serres is also mistaken in saying that all the income from the tax was assigned to Biche and Mouche in part payment for debts owed them by the king. They were given 1/21 of the total income from the tax, *Ord.*, I, 326. The rest was collected by local officials and sent to the Treasury with their general receipts, which explains why Borrelli de Serres found no specific entries under this head in the Journal

the royal domain had long been subject to sales-taxes.[19] In 1292 the government apparently tried to increase the yield from this tax by imposing it on many towns which had not paid it before. This extension of the sales-tax seems to have been general in the north, although it may not have been applied in the southern *sénéchaussées*.[20] Paris paid 100,000 l.t. in installments from 1292 to 1300 to escape this tax.[21] The commune of Provins gave the king 600 l. a year from 1293 to 1297 in return for exemption.[22] Reims,[23] Chalons, Laon, Tournai,[24] La Rochelle, St. Jean d'Angély,[25] Troyes,[26] and Senlis [27]

---

of the Treasury. See B.N., Coll. Clairembault 228, p. 903, account of the seneschal of Beaucaire at St. John's 1303, listing 938 l.t. receipts from this tax at Aigues-Mortes and Nîmes after deducting the share of Biche and Mouche.

[19] Borrelli de Serres, II, 448. A.N., J 892, no. 9, a sales-tax for maintenance of the port had been instituted at Aigues-Mortes by St. Louis.

[20] *H.L.*, X, col. 200, a "maltôte" was ordered in the whole *sénéchaussée* of Beaucaire in 1287. A.N., J 895, no. 6, a protest of Aigues-Mortes against a new sales-tax (they were already paying a local one, see note 19) perhaps refers to this. I have found no other references to this tax and it seems unlikely that it was collected very generally or for a very long period.

[21] E. Boutaric, "Notices et extraits de documents inédits rélatifs à l'histoire de France sous Philippe le Bel," *Notices et extraits des manuscrits*, XX, 2 (1861), pp. 22–25.

[22] M. Prou et J. d'Auriac, *Actes et comptes de la commune de Provins* (Provins, 1933), pp. 89, 93, 95, 98, 166.

[23] Boutaric, *loc. cit.*, p. 23. Reims agreed to pay 10,000 l.t. to avoid the sales-tax.

[24] *Ibid.*, p. 45. Chalons, Laon and Tournai are paying installments in 1295 on a lump sum promised the king to avoid the sales-tax.

[25] A.N., K 496, no. 3, m. 2, La Rochelle pays 12,000 l.t. and St. Jean d'Angély 2000 l.t. to buy off the sales-tax.

[26] *Inventaires des archives departementales*, Aube, *Série* G., III, 215, in 1294 the chapter of Troyes paid "pour raison de la grace dou denier de la livre faite à notre seigneur le Roy."

[27] B.N., Coll. Moreau 212, fol. 36, St. Frambaud of Senlis is paying a fixed sum instead of the sales-tax in 1293.

also preferred to buy off the tax. Yet where the tax was collected, as at Poitiers, the net yield seems remarkably small.[28] Perhaps because of uneven returns, perhaps because the tax could not be imposed on transactions in lands of the nobles,[29] perhaps because of popular opposition,[30] the attempt to extend the sales-tax was abandoned after 1297. Taxes on sales have little importance during the latter part of Philip's reign. In Normandy there seems to have been a special sales-tax collected in sea-ports for defense of the coast, which began in 1299 (or even earlier) and reached its peak in 1302–1303. During the latter two years it was taken at the high rate of fourpence in the pound.[31] It is not mentioned after 1303; it probably ceased when peace was made with Flanders. In 1314 collectors of the new subsidy were instructed to substitute a sales-tax for the tax based on commutation of military service if they

[28] A.N., K 496, no. 3, m. 1, an account of debts owed the king lists only 248 l. 12 s.t. from the sales-tax in Poitiers between 1292 and 1297, only 63 l.t. in Niort, 1290–1297, and only 55 l.t. in St. Maixent for an undetermined period ending in 1297. This account of course does not give a complete record of payments, but if large sums were received from the sales-tax they should have left more of a mark on the list of debts.

[29] E. Boutaric, *Actes du Parlement de Paris* (Paris, 1863), I, 285. Farmers of Norman *prévôtés* complained that they were not getting their expected income from markets because their customers went to the barons' markets which were exempt from the sales-tax. According to this document the general sales-tax was imposed in Normandy in 1292 and was abandoned at Pentecost 1293 because Norman commerce was suffering from raids by the English and the men of Bayonne. The tax in Normandy was taken only on large-scale transactions.

[30] All the chroniclers mention the sales-tax (maltôte) in especially bitter terms, perhaps because it was the first attempt at general taxation during the reign. See *H.F.*, XXI, 205; *ibid.*, XX, 577, 662.

[31] Mignon, nos. 1499, 1657c. *Ibid.*, nos. 1385, 1390, 1393, accounts "obolorum maris," one dated (probably erroneously) 1290. *Olim II*, 374, Rouen gives an aid for the royal galleys, 1294.

thought it advantageous to the king,[32] but few of them did so.[33] Except for the period 1292–1297 the sales-tax was not an important source of revenue for the royal government.

A fourth kind of tax was based on the king's right to control foreign trade. According to the economic ideas of the period, exports impoverished a country, and enriched its enemies. Therefore exports should be discouraged. Both Philip III and Philip IV prohibited the export of wool, cloth, grain, wine, animals, precious metals, and many other things.[34] This list included almost everything which might be produced or manufactured in France. It even included raw materials, such as wool, which might be merely in transit through France.[35] Obviously many merchants would seek permission to export prohibited articles and the government could make money by selling such permissions. We have records only of the grants of the right to export wool and woolen cloth, although permission to export other articles must have been given from time to time. Licenses to export wool were rare under Philip III but became more common in the time of his son.[36] They

[32] Boutaric, "Notices et Extraits," no. 41.

[33] Mignon, no. 1616, a maltôte was taken in parts of Vermandois; *H.F.*, XXI, 570, Provins agreed to the levying of a sales-tax for the subsidy of 1314. But the summary of the subsidy of 1314, *H.F.*, XXI, 567 ff. shows that most other towns fined for lump sums.

[34] *Ord.*, XI, 353; I, 422, 505.

[35] G. Bigwood, "La politique de la laine en France sous les règnes de Philippe le Bel et de ses fils," *Revue Belge*, XV (1936), 79, 429; XVI (1937), 95. This excellent article sums up most of what is known about export dues during this period.

[36] G. Bigwood, *loc. cit.*, XV, 81, 429, found only one license under Philip III.

were not at first an important source of revenue. A license was issued soon after 1285 to merchants of Milan allowing them to export an unlimited amount of wool for six years for 50 s.t. a sack. However, this revenue was assigned to the duke of Burgundy in 1288.[37] In 1287 the Mozzi of Florence were licensed to export wool for three years through the port of Aigues-Mortes. They had to pay 1030 l.t. a year plus 20 s.t. for each four quintals exported.[38] After this concession expired, the Guidi dominated the wool export business for fifteen years. They received a license early in 1291 [39] which was renewed for four years in 1293.[40] There is no record of a renewal in 1297 but in 1303 they were given what seems to be a monopoly of wool exports for two years.[41] There is nothing to show that the Guidi paid the government anything for these licenses. Since Biche and Mouche Guidi were members of the royal household and since the king owed them a great deal of money it seems likely that these licenses were issued in part payment of the king's debt. If the Guidi could export wool free of dues they had a practical monopoly and it is not surprising that no licenses for large-scale exports were sold during this period. Yet there was a small income from exports of wool between 1296 and 1299 [42] which shows

[37] *Ibid.*, 430.

[38] *Ibid.*, 430; B.N., Coll. Doat 155, fol. 196, gives the rate of 30 s.t. for four quintals. Since the later rates ran as high as 70 s.t. for a load of 4 quintals, 30 s.t. does not seem unreasonable, even with the 1030 l.t. annual payment.

[39] Bigwood, *loc. cit.*, XV, 431–433; B.N., Coll. Doat 156, fol. 20.

[40] J. Petit (and others), *Essai de restitution des plus anciens memoriaux de la Chambre des Comptes* (Paris, 1899), nos. 40, 571.

[41] Bigwood, *loc. cit.*, XV, 433; A.N., K 37, no. 15 *ter*.

[42] Robert Fawtier, *Comptes du trésor* (Paris, 1930), p. 14, 437 l.t. from

that merchants must have found it profitable to buy permission to take out a few sacks of wool from time to time. After the death of Biche and Mouche the government seems to have made an effort to increase the revenue from export dues. Licenses to export small quantities of wool may have been issued from time to time,[43] but the bulk of the trade was concentrated in the hands of the Fini of Florence and the community of merchants of Milan. The Fini were licensed in 1308 to export 1000 loads a year for 70 s.t. a load. In 1310 they received a ten-year concession to export 1500 loads a year. They were to pay 50 s.t. a load for sheep's wool and 60 s.t. a load for lamb's wool but had to guarantee a minimum payment to the government of 4250 l.t. a year.[44] The Milanese were permitted in 1308 to export 1100 loads a year, paying 70 s.t. a load. In 1310 they too received a ten-year permit. They could export 2400 loads a year, paying the same rates as the Fini, and guaranteeing a minimum payment of 6000 l.t. a year.[45] Thus the government was assured an income of 10,500 l.t. a year from export dues on wool. Unfortunately the rate was too high to make export profitable, except under very favorable conditions. Even in the last years of Philip the Fair's reign some of the promised payments were in

---

export of wool at Andelot in accounts of All Saints 1296; B.N., ms. lat. 9783, fols. 83 and 19v, 480 l.p. from same source in 1298; *ibid.*, fols. 37, 86, and 109, 696 l.p. from this in 1299.

43 *Olim*, III, 1034, a license to export 200 loads of wool granted in 1308; E. Perroy, "La Fiscalité royale en Beaujolais," *Moyen Âge*, XXXIX (1928), 6, the merchants of Beaujolais were allowed to export wool cloth in 1311 by paying 7 d. in the pound.

44 Bigwood, *loc. cit.*, XV, 434–5; A.N., JJ 45, no. 54.

45 Bigwood, *loc. cit.*, XV, 436; A.N., JJ 42A, no. 84, JJ 45, no. 53.

arrears, and shortly after, both the Fini and the Milanese bought release from their contracts.[46]

Occupational taxes compose the fifth group. Money-lenders were engaged in what was morally and legally a disreputable business and they had to pay large sums for permission to carry on their affairs. French money-lenders were often required to pay subsidies at double the normal rate.[47] Italians who engaged in money-lending,[48] and Jews in general were arrested from time to time by the government and forced to surrender a large part of their capital in return for permission to remain and do business in France. The Italians were forced to pay large sums in this way in 1291–2; one account says that the receipts were 221,000 l.t.[49] They were squeezed again in 1303–4,[50] in 1309–10,[51] and perhaps twice more before the end of the reign [52] but none of the accounts

[46] Bigwood, *loc. cit.*, XVI, 112–116.

[47] A.N., JJ 36, no. 106; *Ord.*, I, 351. B.N., ms. lat. 9783, fols. 75, 17v, Jews of Troyes and Orleans paid a tax of 1/14 of their property in 1298 when everyone else paid 1/50.

[48] Bigwood, *loc. cit.*, XV, 439; A.N., JJ 45, no. 93, the king promises the merchants of Milan in 1310 that all Milanese who are not open usurers will be exempted from ordinances against the Lombards. This shows that the arrests of the Lombards were, at least in theory, caused by their activity as money-lenders.

[49] Mignon, nos. 2073, 2076; B.N., Coll. Doat 51, fol. 1 v.

[50] *Olim*, III, 172. The Lombards were tallaged by Biche and Mouche some time shortly before 1306. Mignon, no. 2053, the Italians fined with a royal agent in 1303–4.

[51] Mignon, no. 2050, the Lombards of France fined with three deputies of the king in 1309–10.

[52] *Ord.*, I, 489–491, 494, the goods and debts of Italians living in France were seized by royal officials in 1311, but they were allowed to redeem them in 1312. Bib. de Rouen, ms. 33401, fol. 109, taxes on Lombards are noted in a roll of 1312. This may be merely a continuation of the operation of 1309–10, though it seems curious that it should have taken so long. Bib. de

of those operations have survived. As for the Jews, they could be tallaged by the king as he saw fit. In the early years of the reign the tallage probably remained at a fixed, rather low rate.[53] In 1290 [54] and again in 1295 [55] efforts seem to have been made to increase income from the tallage of the Jews, but by 1299 receipts from this tax were again rather low.[56] The final confiscation of Jewish property in 1306 might be considered as raising the rate of taxation to 100 per cent: one of the rare cases in which the power to tax actually became the power to destroy. A curious variation of this procedure occurred in Poitou and the French part of Saintonge in 1292. Edward I had expelled the Jews from all English possessions, including Gascony,[57] in

---

Rouen, ms. 33400, fols. 29, 30, 30v (extracts from Journal of the Treasury), many Lombard companies make fine with the king at the end of 1314. They pay sums ranging from 20 to 743 l.t.

[53] R. Fawtier, *Comptes du trésor*, p. xxxi, income from Jews is 2000 l.p. at Candlemas 1288, 5268 l.p. at Candlemas in 1291, and 2720 l.p. at Candlemas 1292. A.N., J 892, no. 9, fol. 4, in Beaucaire the tallage was in proportion to the credits of the Jews. B.N., Coll. Doat 37, fols. 195, 215, the Jews of the South were tallaged every year, 1281–1290.

[54] Fawtier, *loc. cit.*, receipts from Jews at Ascension 1290 were 33,761 l.p., far above normal. Mignon, no. 2113, Biche and Mouche account for a tallage of 80,000 l.p. on the Jews from Candlemas 1281 n.st. (*read* 1291) to All Saints 1292.

[55] *H.L.*, X, cols. 315, 316, the Jews of Beaucaire were arrested early in 1295, their houses were searched and their chattels were seized. Fawtier, *Comptes*, p. 14, there were unusually large receipts from the Jews of the north in 1296.

[56] L. Lazard, "Les revenues tirés des juifs de France (XIIIe siècle)," *Revue des études juives*, XV (1887), 241, finds that income from Jews, including fines, listed in the Journal of the Treasury, was as follows: 7344 l.t. from 21 June 1298 to 18 April 1299; 20,094 l.t. from 3 May 1299 to 12 March 1300; 10,273 l.t. from 4 May 1300 to 3 November 1300.

[57] *Olim*, II, 311.

1290. Charles II of Sicily expelled the Jews from his counties of Anjou and Maine in 1288, and in return was granted three *sous* from each hearth by a council of prelates and nobles.[58] With these examples in mind royal agents succeeded in getting the inhabitants of Saintonge and Poitou to pay a *fouage* at the heavy rate of 6 s.t. a hearth for six years in return for the expulsion of the Jews from those provinces.[59] By 1296 Saintonge had paid 32,997 l.t., while Poitou contributed 26,700 l.t. between 1292 and 1297.[60] However the Jews probably kept their property; at least there is no mention of confiscated Jewish goods in the accounts of Saintonge and Poitou at this time.

Finally, forced loans which were never repaid may be considered a form of taxation. Philip III had borrowed a good deal of money for the war with Aragon, but apparently a real effort was made to repay these loans.[61] Philip the Fair borrowed even more money for the campaigns in Gascony. A very incomplete summary given by Mignon shows that at least 632,000 l.t. was collected,[62] and this includes no loans from Languedoc. These loans were undoubtedly forced. Property of serfs of the Temple was seized in order to make them grant

[58] L. Lazard, "Les juifs de Touraine," *Revue des études juives*, XVII (1888), 225.

[59] *Archives historiques du Poitou*, XLIV (1923), 226.

[60] A.N., K 496, no. 3, m. 1, 2; no. 4, m. 3. Arrears probably came in after this account was made up, which would increase both sums.

[61] A.N., K 496, no. 4, m. 7, 14; B.N., ms. fr. 20683, fols. 3–5v. Mignon, no. 1171.

[62] Mignon, nos. 1106–1163. See Boutaric, "Notices et extraits," p. 45, where the total of loans from "rich burghers" is given as 630,000 l.t. This total is incomplete because many loans came in after it was compiled.

loans,[63] and in Champagne the government found it necessary to send out a special agent to free poor people from the heavy loans which had been assessed against them by the first collectors.[64] Most of these loans were not repaid, at least during the reign of Philip the Fair. *A priori* it might be argued that at no period after 1296 did the government have a large enough surplus to pay off a debt of seven or eight hundred thousand pounds. Existing financial records show that some especially favored individuals, usually clerics or royal officials,[65] were repaid, but the amount which we know was repaid was less than ten per cent of the total. Many men preferred to make small outright gifts to the king in 1294 and 1295 rather than larger loans which they felt would never be repaid.[66] If Mignon's figures can be trusted there were 25,434 l.t. of gifts in Reims and only 1533 l.t. of loans. In Saintonge and Poitou there were 44,910 l.t. of gifts and 5666 l.t. of loans. Elsewhere the proportion was reversed, as in the bailliage of Sens, where there were 25,139 l.t. of loans and 1547 l.t. of gifts.[67] The distrust of government borrowing caused by the events of 1294–1297 is evident in 1302 when new loans were

[63] A.N., K 36B, no. 31.

[64] B.N., ms. lat. 9018, nos. 43, 44; ms. fr. 25992, no. 9.

[65] B.N., ms. lat. 9783, fol. 17, loans of 4483 l.t. repaid to nuns of Prouille by being credited against the tenths which they owed the king, 14 Oct. 1298; *ibid.*, fols. 29v, 115v, loans repaid to *baillis* 4 Jan. 1299, and 30 May 1301; *ibid.*, fols. 123v, 125v, five creditors had assigned their loans to the Franciscans, probably thinking that they would never be paid, but the Franciscans got the money Dec. 1301. See B.N., Coll. Baluze 394, fols. 19, 28, 32, 41, a few loans of 1295 repaid in 1305.

[66] B.N., ms. fr. 25992, no. 9, ten men prefer to give 10 l.t. apiece. The usual loan was 20 to 40 l.t., see ms. lat. 9018, nos. 50–58.

[67] Mignon, nos. 1126, 1159, 1132.

sought. The famous letter of Philip to Jean Clersens, a Treasury official, asking for a loan has often been discussed. The king first cajoles and then threatens, but at the end he promises: "duquel prest vous rendre nous voulens que vous soiez asseurez et assenez tout à vostre devise."[68] Men who were less in the king's power had to be given more specific assurances. The collectors of the loan of 1302 were empowered to pledge local revenues as security for repayment.[69] The income from this loan does not seem to have been very large and it is probable that most of it was repaid. In the last three years of the reign there was a little more borrowing,[70] on what terms is unknown. On the whole the forced loan is important as a means of taxation only in 1294–1297.

None of these taxes could be collected without consulting the people who were taxed. This was true because medieval governments had little information about the numbers and wealth of their subjects. The number of hearths in a town could be found only by consulting the town government; the income or wealth of a landowner could be determined only by consulting the man himself or his neighbors. It is also true that there were never enough government officials to take care of the details of assessment and collection. Even the most oppressive taxes were assessed and collected by the people who paid them. Thus the tallage on the Jews

[68] Boutaric, *La France sous Philippe le Bel* (Paris, 1861), p. 298.

[69] Boutaric, "Notices et extraits," p. 58; A.N., JJ 36, nos. 5, 14.

[70] Bibliothèque de Rouen, mss. 33401 (Leber 5870 t. 4), fol. 109; 33400 (Leber 5870 t. 3), fols. 30–31v.

was collected by Jews [71] and the forced loan was assessed by the burgesses who paid it.[72] Since the government always had to have the cooperation of those who paid there was always a chance for negotiations between the two parties. The form of the tax might be modified, or certain favors might be granted in return for prompt payment. Even the despised Jews were given privileges. Special judges were named for their cases in 1289 and 1292; [73] they were protected from Church courts in 1288; [74] and royal officials were regularly ordered to help them collect their debts.[75] The Lombards received some very valuable privileges in 1295 in return for allowing a sales-tax to be imposed on them. They were freed from all other taxes except those on real estate and given a special legal position which would ensure speedy trials in courts which they preferred.[76]

It is true, of course, that most of the concessions granted by the government had no constitutional, or even political, significance. But the fact that no tax could be collected without negotiating, often with thousands of individuals or communities, was important. A tax which could not be refused could be delayed by

[71] *H.L.*, X, cols. 203, 231, 250; B.N., ms. lat. 9783, fol. 19, a Jew of Rouen turns in the tallage of his fellow-Jews; Lazard, "Revenues tirés des juifs," p. 240, a list of Jews who collected tallage for the king.

[72] A. Longnon, *Documents relatifs au comté de Champagne* (Paris, 1914), III, 119. "Ce sunt li nom des personnes de Troies et de la chastelerie estimées à faire prest à notre seignor le Roy par la commune renommée et par le serment des preudeshomes de la ville de Troies. . . ."

[73] *H.L.*, X, col. 217; IX, 270.

[74] *Ibid.*, X, col. 232.

[75] *Ibid.*, X, col. 250; Ch. V. Langlois, "Formulaires de lettres," *Notices et extraits des manuscrits*, XXXIV, 1 (1891), no. 13.

[76] *Ord.*, I, 326.

endless arguments and conferences, and delay was almost as bad as refusal to a government which was chronically short of money. The frantic letters sent to local officials in 1302 and 1303,[77] when the disaster at Courtrai stimulated the growth of opposition to taxation, show how slow collections could embarrass the government. The opposition to the aid for marrying Isabelle was less serious, but was enough to delay collection of this tax in many regions for three years.[78] It was found inadvisable to repeat taxes which were especially unpopular. Sales-taxes were abandoned, forced loans were abandoned, and taxes for defense were continually modified in an attempt to find a formula which would satisfy everyone.

Moreover, in the case of the two most important taxes, the tenth and the subsidy for war, conditions were imposed which did have constitutional significance. These were the most general taxes; everyone in the kingdom except the very poor paid one or the other. They were the only taxes paid by the privileged classes of clergy and nobility. Naturally they offered the best opportunity to impose restrictions on the government.

The tenths granted by the pope do not concern us.

[77] *Archives historiques du Poitou*, XIII, nos. 189, 191, 196, 198; A.N., JJ 36, fols. 1–9 and nos. 85, 97, 125, 164, 177, 184.

[78] A.N., JJ 42A, no. 138, this aid due in 1308 was being collected in Limousin only in 1311; Mignon, nos. 1573–75, it was assessed in Poitou, Saintonge, Limousin and Angoulême only in 1310; *Mémoires de la Société Académique du Nivernais*, III (1888), 55, the aid was collected in Bourges in 1311; *Archives anciennes de la ville de St. Quentin*, ed. E. Lemaire (St. Quentin, 1888), nos. 220–224, St. Quentin refused to pay the sum assessed against it for this aid. Officials had to seize property of merchants to get partial payment in 1310. Argument was still going on over the remainder in 1311 and it is doubtful if it was ever paid.

Conditions imposed in these grants were the result of a treaty between two sovereign powers. The clergy who paid these tenths did not consent to them and could not ask for political concessions in return for paying them. They could only suggest to the pope that he ask certain favors for them during his negotiations with the king. But the pope, quite naturally, was more interested in international politics than in the internal affairs of France and the French clergy gained very little by the conditions which he imposed.

When, on the other hand, the king ignored the pope and asked his clergy directly for a grant he was in a very weak position. Until 1297 it was against canon law for the clergy to give the king money without consulting the pope.[79] Even when Boniface VIII removed this restriction, after the great quarrel over the bull *Clericis Laicos* it was still difficult to force the clergy to pay. According to the new rule, in a great emergency the king could tax the clergy for the defense of the realm without consulting the pope.[80] Nothing was said about obtaining the consent of the French Church, and on at least one occasion a tax was arbitrarily imposed on a province which had refused to grant it freely.[81] Yet while Philip's ministers were not afraid to put a good deal of pressure on churchmen in order to get taxes, they usually found it advisable to negotiate with assemblies of the clergy and to make concessions in return for grants. The French government was ruthless and compara-

79 E. Chénon, *Histoire générale du droit français* (Paris, 1926), I, 914.

80 *Ibid.*, 935.

81 A.N., J 350, nos. 5, 6, royal officials impose and collect a tenth by force in the province of Tours, 1305.

tively strong, but it could not ignore public opinion. It could control public opinion to some extent by unscrupulous propaganda, but propaganda was expensive and time-consuming. The affair of the Temple, for example, dragged on for five years and required an endless number of embassies, assemblies, letters and proclamations. It was wiser not to overwork the propaganda machine. Moreover the clergy still had a hold on the people. While secularism was growing in France it was still unpopular to fail to give external signs of respect to the Church. During the quarrels with Boniface VIII the strategy of the government was to make it appear that they were attacking Boniface as a person and not the Church as an institution. They needed the neutrality, if not the support of the French Church, but this could not be obtained if the clergy were angered over questions of taxation. For these reasons it was advisable to avoid head-on collisions with the French clergy and to make some of the concessions they demanded when they were asked for tenths. It is probably no accident that all the important ordinances in favor of the Church came before 1305. After that date the government abandoned its attempt to tax the clergy directly and reverted to the old practice of getting grants from the pope.

There is more direct evidence than the dates of ordinances to show the demands which the Church made in return for grants of taxes. In 1294 the government decided, for the first time, to deal directly with the French clergy. The pope had just refused a tenth [82] and the expense of the occupation of Gascony was already

[82] Chénon, I, 915; *H. L.*, IX, 159.

noticeable. The first plan seems to have been to assemble a national council of the French clergy at Paris but orders to this effect were countermanded.[83] The official excuse was the desire to spare the prelates expense, but the government may have also wished to weaken opposition by dividing it. Provincial councils were summoned by royal authority [84] and these councils granted the king a tenth for two years. But they also attached conditions to their grants, conditions which resembled each other so closely as to suggest that they had been drawn up and circulated before the meetings by the leaders of the clergy. The council held at Aurillac for the province of Bourges, 29 September 1294, conceded a tenth for two years "sub modo . . . ac conditionibus infra scriptis": [85]

1. The consent of the pope must be had, unless the peril is so great that it cannot be awaited.
2. If peace comes or a truce is made collection of the tenth is to cease.
3. If the pope should grant a tenth or other levy this tenth shall not be collected.
4. The tenth is to be collected by ecclesiastics and not by royal officials.
5. All money current in the place taxed is to be accepted.
6. The clergy are to be free from military service, con-

[83] *H.L.*, X, col. 302; L. Ménard, *Histoire de Nismes* (Paris, 1750), I, *preuves*, 128, 130, letters to the bishop of Uzés, and the clergy of Le Puy countermanding summons to the king's presence and ordering provincial councils.

[84] A.N., J 456, no. 31, J 712, no. 302[12], two royal agents were apparently traveling through the Midi, summoning one local council after another to grant the tenths. The references in note 83 also show that the councils were summoned by the king or his agents.

[85] A.N., J 1035, no. 38.

tributions for military service or any other subsidy, and from levies by nobles in return for this grant.

7. The king must send each prelate a letter stating that he understands that this grant is "ex sola gratia et mera liberalitate."

An assembly of the exempt clergy of the province of Narbonne at Béziers, 28 October 1294,[86] and one of the exempt of Bourges at Clermont, 8 November 1294 made their grants on the same conditions.[87] The clergy of Brittany met at Saumur, 5 October 1294, and set much the same conditions, omitting the first and fifth clauses and using a weaker form of the sixth.[88] A council for the rest of the province of Tours met at the same time and place and made the same sort of grant.[89] In addition, the bishop of Angers drew up a long list of grievances against royal officials and sent it to the king. This is one of the most outspoken attacks on the government during the whole reign. It complained of the conduct of collectors of the tenth, of collectors of fines for mortmain, of the custodians of *regalia*, and of interferences with the Church's rights of justice by secular officials. It wound up with what was almost a threat of rebellion. The king was warned that no prince could win a war who was at odds with his subjects, that he was oppressing the Church as Pharaoh oppressed the Jews and he was invited to contemplate the fate of Rehoboam.[90] The supposedly treasonous utterances of

86 A.N., J 712, no. 302[12].

87 A.N., J 456, no. 31.

88 A.N., J 1035, no. 39. The sixth clause was weakened by making it cover only additional levies by the nobles.

89 C. Port, "Le Livre de Guillaume le Maire," *Collection de documents inédits sur l'histoire de France, Mélanges historiques,* II (Paris, 1877), p. 320.

90 *Ibid.*, pp. 322 ff.

the bishop of Pamiers a few years later were no worse than this. Yet this letter, which did not even formally impose conditions on the grant of the tenth, met a prompt response. Letters were rushed to all royal officials forbidding the practices of which the bishop had complained.[91]

The council of the province of Lyons which met at Mâcon, 8 February 1295, followed the lead of the earlier assemblies. They asked for everything requested by the council of Aurillac (except clauses one and five) and in addition demanded redress for all injuries inflicted on ecclesiastical persons by royal officials.[92] The specially privileged Premonstratensians [93] and Cluniacs [94] made separate grants with similar reservations.

Even though these councils nominally represented all the clergy of France [95] there were protests against their acts. The chapter of Laon appealed to the pope in its effort to avoid paying the tenth while the Cistercians of Beaucaire allowed their property to be seized by the seneschal rather than make the required contribution.[96] The government seems to have been worried by this opposition and elaborate preparations were made to as-

[91] Port, pp. 331–334, seven letters of Philip's, dated 10 November 1294, forbid specifically acts which had caused the bishop's protest.

[92] A.N., J 1035, no. 36.

[93] *Ibid.*, no. 37.

[94] A.N., J 938, no. 38. See A.N., J 746, no. 3, a similar (undated) grant by Marmoutier. On the whole the exempt orders imposed fewer conditions than the ordinary clergy.

[95] Mignon, no. 701, a council for Bordeaux was held at Pons; A.N., JJ 34, fol. 49 and one for Reims at Compiègne in addition to those already mentioned.

[96] Georges Digard, *Philippe le Bel et le Saint Siège* (Paris, 1936), I, 256, 257.

sure a good reception to the next demand for money. Almost a year before the grant of 1294 expired commissioners were sent to a council of the province of Narbonne (and probably to other provincial councils as well) with power to offer extensive privileges to the clergy of that region in return for four tenths. The council felt that the king was asking too much and offering too little, so they sent two delegates to Philip to ask greater liberties, authorizing them to concede a tenth for two or three years if their requests were granted. Before the delegates reached the king a copy of the bull *Clericis Laicos* was received by their archbishop. This bull forbade, in sweeping terms, all contributions by the clergy to lay governments, and the archbishop had to send an express messenger to his delegates, ordering them to make no grant to the king. The delegates went on to meet Philip, and explained the situation to him, protesting the good-will of the province and throwing all the blame on the pope. The king offered them satisfaction for all their demands if they could find a way of making a grant without violating the papal prohibition. The delegates, of course, could not do this, and negotiations ended at this point.[97]

Boniface always claimed that *Clericis Laicos* was not directed specifically against the French government, and there is no reason to doubt his word. Lay taxation

[97] *Abhandlung der Historischen Classe der Königlich Bayerischen Akademie der Wissenschaften*, III Band, Abth. III (1841), "Processus factus . . . super zelo quem habuit d. Philippus Franciae Rex in petendo convocari concilium super haeresi imposita d. Bonifacio Papa VIII," ed. C. Höfler, pp. 75–6. Bérenger, cardinal bishop of Tusculum, who was bishop of Béziers in 1296 and one of the delegates sent by the council to Philip, told this story at length in his deposition.

of the clergy was an issue everywhere, and the French clergy were not alone in appealing to the pope against such exactions. In fact the bull came at the worst possible time for the French Church. The government was ready to make large concessions in return for a grant. Boniface stopped these negotiations, but the net result of his interference was that the French clergy paid more and secured less than if he had not interfered. He was sincere in wishing to stop taxation of the Church, but he was deeply involved in political intrigues in Italy and Germany. He could not carry out his plans in those two countries without the support of the French government and in the end the French clergy were sacrificed to diplomatic exigencies.

There is no need to repeat Digard's masterful demonstration of the way in which the French government put pressure on the pope.[98] Externally advantage was taken of the confused situation in Italy and especially of the revolt of the Colonna. Within France the clergy were accused of selfishness and treachery in failing to aid in the defense of the realm. Under the prodding of Pierre Flote the archbishops of Reims, Sens, Narbonne and Rouen begged Boniface to suspend *Clericis Laicos* in France.[99] This was followed by a specific request, 31 January 1297, for permission to make a grant for defense of the realm. The request seems to have been drawn up by a sort of council at Paris, composed of the archbishops of Reims, Sens, and Rouen, and some of their suffragans.[100] Boniface felt that it was wise to

[98] Digard, I, 246–345.

[99] P. Dupuy, *Histoire du differend d'entre le pape Boniface VIII et Philippe le Bel* (Paris, 1655), *preuves*, p. 26; Digard, I, 268–9. [100] Digard, I, 305.

yield and on 28 February 1297 gave the French clergy permission to aid the king. In the circumstances this was practically an order to pay, and the French Church, already suffering from the hostility and suspicion which the government had stirred up, did not hesitate to make the grant. A very full council of the Church held at Paris on 27 and 28 March granted a double tenth, with only three unimportant reservations. The tenth was to cease if the war ended; it was to be collected only by churchmen; and no other burden was to be imposed on the clergy.[101] This was bad enough, but worse was to follow. For on 31 July 1297 the pope retreated completely from the position established in *Clericis Laicos*. By the bull *Etsi de Statu* the king was empowered to ask aid whenever, in his judgment, the realm was in danger.[102] This collapse of papal opposition so discouraged the French Church that it failed to realize that tenths could not be easily collected without its acquiescence, and that it could still impose conditions when it made grants. Not only was the double tenth collected without difficulty in 1297 but the government succeeded in having it prolonged for a year by a council which met at Paris. The clergy were still too stunned to do much bargaining and no important requests were made on this occasion.[103] In fact, Mignon, writing a generation later,

[101] *Ibid.*, I, 308, seven archbishops and forty bishops sealed the act. *Cf.* Mignon, no. 712, "Decima duplex . . . concessa fuit regi Philippo Pulcro a papa Bonifacio VIII ad requisitionem prelatorum. . . ."

[102] Chénon, p. 935; Digard, I, 341.

[103] *Codex Dunensis*, ed. J. B. M. C. Kervyn de Lettenhove (Bruxelles, 1875), p. 275, the abbot of Clairvaux announces with great sorrow that at a council at Paris the order of Citeaux, "coactus" by the pope's letter, granted a double tenth.

spoke of this double tenth of 1298 as "imposed" by the king and failed to mention the formal assent of the council.[104]

The government apparently thought that the tenths were now established as regular payments. When the double tenth of 1298 had been collected it immediately asked for a new grant. Councils held in 1299 at Paris, Lyons, and perhaps elsewhere, conceded a tenth for two years.[105] Philip was still on good terms with the pope, and he had been very successful in his war against England and Flanders, so he was not afraid to threaten the Paris assembly with a forced levy at a high rate, if they refused to grant the tenth.[106] In these circumstances it is not surprising that we do not hear of conditions being imposed. It is possible, however, that the important privileges for the provinces of Rouen, Narbonne, and Bordeaux, and the diocese of Mende, issued in March 1300 (n.st.) were the result of requests made at these councils. These privileges, while not identical, have many points in common, which suggest that the clergy had organized a joint protest against the conduct of royal officials. All four documents state that churchmen are not to be cited in lay courts, that full credit is to be given to letters sealed by prelates and their of-

104 Mignon, no. 712.

105 Mignon, no. 766, mentions only a council at Lyons. But *Codex Dunensis*, p. 524, speaks of a council at Paris, 9 February 1299, at which "all" prelates, abbots, etc. granted a tenth for two years. These councils may have been for the North and South respectively, although such a division for ecclesiastical purposes was not customary. It is also possible that they were provincial councils and that others were held of which we know nothing.

106 *Codex Dunensis*, p. 524. The king is reported to have said that if the clergy would not make the grant freely "posset si vellet, virtute regia et privilegialiter fecisse quod forte nobis fuisset intolerabile et dampnosum."

ficials, that the temporalities of bishops are to be seized only by royal order and then only partially, that abuses in the collection of annates are to be stopped, and that the number of royal sergeants is to be diminished.[107] These privileges may have been a reward for the prompt action of the councils of 1299. However, the tenths granted that year were never fully collected. The case of Bernard Saisset caused a new quarrel between France and Rome, and late in 1301 the pope forbade the clergy to pay any more money to the king. This order was applied immediately and since, as usual, collections had been slow, the government lost almost a full year of the two-year grant of 1299.[108] The province of Bordeaux and the diocese of Chartres paid for a year and a half, but the rest of the province of Sens and the provinces of Reims, Bourges, Rouen, Narbonne, Lyons and Auch paid only for one year.[109]

It was hard enough to keep the French clergy on the king's side during the remainder of the struggle with Boniface without adding to the difficulty by new requests for tenths. But by the middle of 1303 the government could hold its hand no longer. The disaster of Courtrai had to be avenged and there was desperate

[107] *Ord.*, I, 334 for Rouen (3 March 1300 n.st.); XI, 390 for Mende (3 March 1300 n.st.); XII, 338, separate letters for the archbishop, and for the other prelates of the province of Narbonne (3 March 1300 n.st); *Gallia Christiana*, II, *Instrumenta* 295, for Bordeaux (3 March 1300 n.st.).

[108] Mignon, no. 766, says that this tenth was never fully collected "propter inhibitionem papae." The Journal of the Treasury (B.N., ms. lat. 9783) shows how collections had been lagging. The Treasury received only 33,523 l.t. from the tenth between 29 April and 5 November 1301. Making all allowances for the incompleteness of these entries and my own errors this is still only one third or one fourth of what might have been expected.

[109] Mignon, nos. 767–779.

need for money. A council of the clergy was summoned at Paris early in the summer [110] and asked for a grant. This council may well have met at the same time as the assembly which was called to accuse Boniface VIII. In any case the war was not going well and the struggle with the pope was becoming desperate. The clergy could ask a high price for their aid and they knew it. They drew up a long document criticizing the royal administration and requesting important concessions in return for their grant.[111] First they suggested that the character of seneschals, *baillis* and other local officials might be improved and that the recent ordinance for the reform of the realm should be enforced. Then they asked for a permanent body of judges at Paris who would settle cases during the whole year without delay. Apparently this request contemplated enlarging the functions of the *maîtres des requêtes*. As for pecuniary aid, they granted a twentieth of their income under the same conditions as those which accompanied an earlier grant of a subsidy on lay property by the prelates and barons.[112] They added the request that if the twentieth were used to restore coins to their former fine-

[110] The date of this council is doubtful. It was after March 1303 (n.st.) because the grant made at the council (Appendix II) refers to the subsidy granted then. It was before 21 August because the king speaks then of "decimam olim nobis concessam," *Ord.*, I, 382. The most likely date is 13–14 June 1303 or soon after, since many prelates at that time attended the assembly which accepted the articles of accusation against Boniface VIII.

[111] Appendix II, *infra*.

[112] *Ord.*, I, 370. These conditions were that no other subsidy, loan, or military service should be asked during the coming year, that no provisions should be seized by royal officials except on cash payment, and that if an aid were granted for reforming of the currency those who paid the present subsidy should be exempt from that levy. 30 March 1303 (n.st.).

ness, a plan which the government had in mind during part of 1303,[113] the change be made only after due warning. If, however, the king wanted a full tenth, new and more important conditions were made. All acquisitions of the Church to date, for which they had not already made fine, were to be amortized gratis. All men might give small sums to the Church to found chaplaincies or anniversary celebrations without fining for permission to amortize. All prelates who paid the extra twentieth were to be free from all military services. Letters were to be given admitting that the king had had no right to take fines for military service from men of the prelates and promising not to do so in the future. Finally they insisted that the debased currency be reformed and that the king should take an oath never to alter the money again "sine magna et inevitabile necessitate." The king would have to pledge his faith, and the members of his secret council would have to take an oath that such necessity existed, and their act would have to be ratified by the great barons and prelates.

These demands were important in themselves. As possible precedents for constitutional government they are even more significant. If the grant of a tenth could be used as an excuse to modify the institutions of the country, as in the proposal for increasing the functions of the *maîtres des requêtes*, then there were no limits to the influence which upper-class tax-payers might have on the government. If the prelates could insist that a fixed constitutional procedure must be followed in order to alter the currency it would not be long before

[113] *Ibid.*, I, 370, 378, 379, 389.

no important act could be done except in this way. The theory implicit in this document is that the great council of prelates and barons shall really have a voice in the government and that their assent shall no longer be an empty form. It is very like the theory of the English magnates during the reign of Henry III and it is expressed in very much the same way.

The government realized the dangers in the conditions which accompanied this grant, and in spite of its desperate need of money, refused at first to consider it.[114] By August it could no longer avoid some concessions. A few prelates were hastily assembled and agreed to pay a tenth,[115] but in return they were allowed only two of the requests which they had made. No charge was to be made for amortizing any property which the Church had recently acquired and no military service, fines for military service, or subsidies for the army were to be asked during that year from any churchman who paid the tenth.[116] This was not a bad bargain, though

[114] *Ord.*, I, 382, the king asks that the tenth "olim concessam," now be paid in return for "gratiis infrascriptis"; A.N., J 231, Amiens no. 10, a letter to the king from the bishop and chapter of Amiens says that "illa concessio decime et vicesime ad plenum Parisius facta non fuisset quia conditiones quas petebant prelati concedere noluistis. . . ."

[115] *Ord.*, I, 382. ". . . nonnullos archiepiscopos et episcopos dicti regni ad nostram presentiam . . . evocatos requiri fecimus ut nobis . . . decimam olim nobis cum dimidia decima ab eis et aliis prelatis sub certa forma pro dicti regni deffensione concessam presencialiter exhiberent, predicta dimidia decima alias congruo tempore persolvenda. . . ." 21 August 1303. This letter speaks of three twentieths, while the conditional grant which I have been discussing mentions only two. However, as is explained in Appendix II, we have the conditional grant only in the form of a draft and it is possible that the prelates, realizing the importance of their demands, or under governmental pressure, increased the amount offered by a twentieth.

[116] *Ibid.*, 382; J. Roucaute and M. Saché, *Lettres de Philippe le Bel réla-*

it was less than the Church had asked. Royal officials demanded large sums for amortization and it was evident that a new subsidy would soon be needed. It might well be cheaper to pay a tenth than to be burdened with these other charges. But though it was not a bad bargain it was not what the clergy as a whole had asked, and there may have been a protest against yielding on any of the conditions.[117] Perhaps because of this opposition, perhaps because it felt it could get more money in other ways, the government soon broke the bargain. In October a new subsidy was asked from all subjects, including churchmen. This flatly contradicted the August agreement, as the government tacitly admitted by immediately announcing that it preferred to have the clergy pay the subsidy rather than the tenth. No further attempts to collect the tenth were made and sums already paid were applied to reduce the amount of subsidy owed by the Church.[118]

---

tives au pays de Gévaudan (Mende, 1896), no. 17; A.N., JJ 36, no. 111, these promises were made to the bishops of Amiens, Angoulême and Mende, to the exempt clergy of Noyon, and probably to all other prelates and communities.

117 A.N., J 231, Amiens no. 10, the clergy of Amiens protested that they owed no tenth because the king had not accepted all the conditions. However they were forced to engage themselves to pay 1500 l.t. of the debts of Valois, the king's brother, to be credited against their tenth. When the attempt to collect the tenth was abandoned they were left with this debt. *Inventaire des archives départementales*, Aveyron, série G., p. 169, the clergy of Rodez protested at some time in 1303 against the king's demands for a tenth.

118 *H.L.*, X, col. 420, letter of Philip to the count of Foix (collector of the subsidy in Languedoc) containing these instructions, 26 October 1303. A.N., J 231, Amiens no. 10, the clergy of Amiens knew that all other churches were freed from the tenth by 10 November 1303.

The retreat of the government was only temporary. Early in 1304 a new campaign was begun to obtain the grant of a tenth. Provincial councils were held at different times and places, perhaps with the idea of weakening resistance to the government's demands. The clergy of Narbonne met at Béziers in February,[119] those of Bourges at Clermont, 11 March,[120] those of Reims at Senlis about 12 April,[121] those of Sens, Tours and Rouen at some time before 15 June.[122] But the prelates had not forgotten their program of 1303. The provincial council of Narbonne obtained an important grant of privileges in February 1304 (n.st.). All their rights of justice were guaranteed, all their acquisitions to that date were amortized gratis, they were given the right to acquire any land needed for church buildings in the future without paying for amortization, and royal claims to *regalia* in the province were surrendered.[123] The clergy of Bourges asked even more. In a document very like that of 1303 they offered one tenth on condition that good money be restored at the king's expense, that all earlier promises to prelates and barons be en-

[119] *H.L.*, IX, 266, 269, 274. According to Mignon, no. 782, the clergy of Lyons met with those of Narbonne.

[120] Mignon, no. 788; A.N., J 1025, no. 4.

[121] *Ord.*, I, 409, letters of the king asking the clergy of Reims for a grant are dated 12 April 1304.

[122] A.N., JJ 36, no. 187, letters of the king, 27 July 1304, asking the prelates of Sens, Reims, Bourges, Tours and Rouen to hurry payment of the tenth they have promised, and referring to recent concessions which he had made. These concessions are almost surely those of 15 June, see below, p. 40. Mignon, nos. 794, 795 seems to indicate that the meetings in Rouen and Sens took place later, but I think he refers to a second set of meetings held to consider royal concessions, see below, p. 41.

[123] *Ord.*, I, 403.

forced, that no further subsidy for the war be asked, and that the pope's consent be obtained. If this was not enough they offered two tenths, on even more stringent conditions. Good money must be restored at the king's expense. All the Church's privileges and all her rights of justice must be respected. All property willed to the Church and all land acquired for church buildings, hospitals or cemeteries was to be retained without paying for amortization. All churchmen (even married clerks living clerically) and all men of the prelates living in lands where they had high justice were to be free from all service and subventions owed for the present war. Clergymen who owed feudal service to the king were to be exempt from it while the tenths were being collected. Royal letters of protection were not to be used to deprive the Church of jurisdiction. Bishops and abbots were not to be punished for acts of their subordinates. No tenth granted by the pope was to be collected before these tenths were paid. No money should be paid the king until he sealed a letter confirming all these points.[124]

Judging by the sequel, the other councils must have made very nearly the same requests. In most provinces the prelates and great exempt monasteries agreed to pay two tenths, while the rest of the clergy paid one.[125] In return for this grant of money the king issued individual charters of privileges to the bishops and exempt abbots.[126] Less inclusive charters were sent to cathe-

[124] A.N., J 1025, no. 4.

[125] Mignon, nos. 782 (Reims), 784 (Narbonne and Lyon), 788 (Bourges), 792 (Tours), 793 (Auch).

[126] *Ord.*, I, 406, and XII, 357 (Reims); V, 632 (Mende); XII, 358 (Lyons

dral chapters and ordinary monasteries, probably because they paid less.[127] The first letters were written early in May for the clergy of the province of Reims; all the others bear the date 15 June. This suggests that the requests of the provincial council of Reims, following those of Bourges, convinced the government that large concessions must be made to the clergy, that a charter was drawn up for Reims alone, and that when it proved satisfactory to the clergy there, it was extended to the rest of the realm.

In these letters of May and June 1304 most of the earlier conditions of the clergy were satisfied. The king promised to reform the currency during the coming year. All acquisitions of the Church to date, and all future acquisitions of land for church buildings or cemeteries were to be amortized without charge. Subjects of chuchmen were not to be allowed to transfer their allegiance to the king and ecclesiastical jurisdiction was not to be troubled by pretext of royal "guard" over the churches. Nothing was to be taken from serfs of the Church when the current lay subsidy was collected and earlier levies on them were to work no prejudice. If the pope granted the king a tenth it was not to be collected until the tenths granted by the French clergy

---

and Bordeaux); XV, 454 (Autun); A.N., K 37, no. 30 (St. Denis); *Gallia Christiana*, I, *Instrumenta*, 11, 32 (Albi, Cahors); II, *Instrumenta* 238 (Le Puy); XIV, *Instrumenta* 24 (St. Mâlo); B.N., Coll. Moreau 218, fols. 43, 52 (Paris and Cluny).

[127] *Ord.*, IV, 344 (Eschaalis); V, 248 (Valloire); XIII, 412 (dean and chapter of Chalons); P. Varin, *Archives administratives de la ville de Reims* (Paris, 1839–43), II, 46, 48 (chapter of Reims and St. Rémi); A.N., JJ 37, no. 16 (Ste. Marie de Soissons); *ibid.*, K 37B, no. 31 (chapter of Laon); B.N., Coll. Moreau 218, fols. 59, 61, 64, 76, 78, 80, 82 (various monasteries).

were paid. Collection of the tenths was to cease if peace or truce were made. Special auditors were to be appointed to hear and remedy all grievances of the Church.[128]

These were large concessions, even if they carefully avoided the constitutional issues raised in the document of 1303. Large as they were, they did not satisfy all the clergy. Apparently new meetings were held to decide whether the king had met the requirements of the clergy. The ecclesiastics of Rouen did not allow the grant to be collected until 1306 and then restricted it to a single tenth on all churchmen.[129] As will be seen below, opposition to the lay subsidy of 1304 was also strong in Rouen. The clergy of Sens permitted collection only in 1305 and likewise paid only a single tenth.[130] In Tours there was an open conflict. The king wrote a long letter in October 1305 arguing that the clergy should pay the double tenth which he asked. He reminded them that they were all part of the body politic, that they owed aid to others in the realm, and wound up with a threat to take the money by force.[131] Yet the archbishop and chapter of Tours and the abbey of St. Martin refused to pay more than a single tenth. Royal officials asserted the king's unqualified right to tax any-

128 The shorter form for the ordinary clergy omitted the promise to reform the coinage, the right to acquire land for church buildings, and the exemption of church serfs from the subsidy.

129 Mignon, no. 795.

130 *Ibid.*, no. 794.

131 A.N., J 350, no. 5. "Novistis plenius qualiter omnes et singuli clerici et laici regni nostri tanquam membra simul in uno corpore vere vivencia sibi debent ad invicem compati mutuumque sibi prestare teneretur auxilium spiritualiter et temporaliter ad conservationem, deffensionem, et custodiam unitatis ipsius regni. . . ."

one for defense of the realm [132] and seized the temporal property of the archbishop. Apparently there was a feeling that an example must be made of someone, for the collectors admitted that there was more profit in a single tenth paid freely than in a double tenth taken by force. The government was still asking damages and seeking to punish the archbishop in 1307.[133]

The events of 1303–04 mark the peak of clerical resistance to taxation during this reign. The election of a friendly pope in 1305 and the ending of the Flemish war freed the government from the necessity of further negotiations with the French clergy. Theoretically it should have been easier to deal with the French Church, which was more or less subject to the king, than with the pope, who was independent. Experience had shown, however, that the French clergy made more embarrassing demands than any pope. It was better for the government to get its grants from the pope even if he demanded a share of the proceeds. With the pressure of war removed the government could afford the extra time needed for negotiations with the papacy, especially as there seems to have been a deliberate policy of easing taxation after 1305. All tenths after 1304 were conceded by the pope. Benedict XI had granted a tenth for two years in 1304, to be effective when good money was restored. This tenth was collected only in 1307 and 1308.[134] Clement V granted a tenth in 1310,

[132] A.N., J 350, no. 5, ". . . tanquam rex et princeps auctoritate sua potest facere impositiones super quascumque personas regni sui et eas capere et levare, specialiter in casu necessitatis. . . ."

[133] *Ibid.*, nos. 5, 6, 7.

[134] Mignon, no. 796.

another in 1312, and a tenth for six years, beginning in 1313, for the Crusade.[135] As usual when pope and king were in accord, the French clergy gained no important concessions on these occasions.

The French Church was unable to impose permanent restrictions on the royal power of taxation, though it did obtain temporary concessions. Owners of lay property were somewhat more successful in trying to limit the king's right to impose a general subsidy for the defense of the realm.

The first general levy on laymen after 1285 was the aid for the knighting of the king. It had been imposed during his father's lifetime, as a means of getting additional resources for the Aragon Crusade, but it was not fully collected until 1286. It seems to have been assessed, in the traditional way, only on those holding directly of the king. Various individuals and communities protested that their privileges freed them from paying such an aid, but they were all directly subject to the crown.[136] Only in the South does there seem to have been an attempt to take the aid from rear-vassals as well as from tenants of the crown. The nobles of Rouergue protested against this practice in October 1285, and the king ordered that the aid be taken only from his immediate vassals. Money collected in violation of this rule was returned.[137]

[135] *Ibid.*, nos. 815, 828, 838. The profits of one year of the six year tenth were reserved for the pope. Though the Crusade never took place the tenth was fully collected, *ibid.*, nos. 839–862.

[136] *Olim*, II, 249, towns held in *paréage* with monasteries do not have to pay the aid for knighting the king, although purely royal towns such as Lorris must pay in spite of their charters.

[137] *H.L.*, X, cols. 192, 248.

A much more important tax was collected in the South in 1294. When it became evident that the dispute with Edward I was likely to lead to war, the feudal levies of the southern provinces were summoned. Fines for default were taken from those who did not appear, and many communes paid large sums to secure exemption from military service.[138] All this had been normal practice under Louis IX and Philip III.[139] But the occupation of Gascony was an expensive operation and more money was needed. The government did what it always did during this reign; it generalized and nationalized an existing custom. The obligation of military service had been steadily extended during the thirteenth century, and the theory had gradually developed that all inhabitants of France were bound to aid the king to defend the realm.[140] Now this theory was to be tested, first in the South, and then throughout the country. And, strangely enough, it was to be tested in its most extreme form. The aid to be demanded was financial rather than personal, although most subjects who admitted their obligation probably thought of it in terms of military service. No great effort was made to

[138] A.N., K 496, no. 3, m. 8v, 9v, fines were taken in Périgord for failure to serve in the army in 1293 and 1294. Montauban and Cahors each paid 500 l.; *ibid.*, no. 4, m. 9, fines in Quercy by Midsummer, 1294 totaled 2430 l., of which 1000 l. was paid by the consuls of Moissac.

[139] C. Stephenson, "Les aides des villes françaises," *Moyen Âge*, XXXIII (1922), 321, 325–328.

[140] J. Declareuil, *Histoire générale du droit français* (Paris, 1925), pp. 706–7; Philippe de Beaumanoir, *Coutumes de Beauvaisis*, ed. A. Salmon, (Paris, 1900), II, 261–2 (no. 1510); "Mes ou tans de guerre ou tans que l'en se doute de guerre . . . li rois puet faire nouveaus establissements pour le commun pourfit de son roiaume: si comme il peut commander . . . que chascuns soit appareillés de mouvoir quant li rois le commandera."

make the tax appear a substitute for personal service, though this was certainly the theory behind the tax in the South, and perhaps in the country as a whole. The men at the head of the government in 1294 must have felt very sure of their strength.

Early in 1294 the constable, who commanded the southern army, asked 6 s.t. from each hearth to meet the expenses of his troops. This request may have been accompanied, in some cases, with a general summons to come to the army. We know that the Majorcan part of Montpellier received such a summons in this year and it seems likely that the count of Foix was told that the hearth-tax was to take the place of general military service.[141] However it is not certain that less independent lords were given this explanation, and in any case the transition was very brusque. The count of Foix, the most powerful baron of the South, was given no opportunity to furnish actual service, or to suggest his own terms for exemption. Instead he was ordered to send representatives at once to the seneschal of Carcassonne to give account of the number of hearths in his domains. They might offer a lump sum instead of the exact product of the tax, but there was to be no escape from paying some money to the government.[142] It is

[141] *Archives de la ville de Montpellier*, ed. F. Castets et J. Berthelé (Montpellier, 1895), I, 148, no. 1996, the Majorcan part of Montpellier received a summons to send soldiers in 1294, which it refused to obey. B.N., Coll. Doat 176, fol. 1 ff., the count of Foix, in protesting against the demand for a subsidy, based his argument on the fact that his subjects were not bound to serve in the royal army, while the seneschal insisted that they were. This shows that the count was asked to pay *fouage* as a substitute for military service.

[142] B.N., Coll. Doat 176, fol. 1.

not surprising that the count protested violently against such an innovation. Yet as far as we can tell his protest had no effect, and in general the tax seems to have been collected. Even so independent a town as Narbonne paid.[143]

More money was needed in 1295, but this time the royal agents in the South made more of an effort to avoid opposition. An assembly of nobles was held in the *sénéchaussée* of Beaucaire to consider taxation,[144] and similar meetings may have taken place elsewhere. The Beaucaire assembly adopted a proposition of the seneschal that a contribution of one and a half per cent be levied on all real estate for support of the army. Values were to be determined by four to six local assessors, acting under the orders of the lord of the district.[145] It is probable that a similar tax was levied in the other southern provinces (Toulouse, Carcassonne, Périgord, Quercy and Rouergue) since they did not contribute to the general subsidy of a hundredth which the rest of the kingdom paid during 1295.[146]

Perhaps the success of a general tax in the South encouraged the government to try a similar measure in

[143] B.N., Coll. Doat 51, fol. 29. *H.L.*, IX, 175, Beaucaire gave 400 l.t. to be freed from the tax.

[144] *H.L.*, IX, 181; B.N., ms. lat. 9192, fol. 61, a protest of the lieutenant of the king of Majorca at Montpellier against the tax speaks of "ordinationem quam dixistis vos fecisse pro tuhitione et deffensione regni Francie de consilio et providencia baronum et nobilium dicte senescallie seu maioris partis eorum nuper per vos apud Vivarium . . . ad hoc specialiter vocatorum . . . ," 20 April 1295.

[145] *Ibid.*, the rate was 30 l. for a "patrimony" (which I take to mean real estate) of 2000 l., and in the same proportion for smaller estates.

[146] Mignon, nos. 1261–1266, found no account for the hundredth of 1295 for those districts.

the rest of the kingdom. Early in 1295 [147] all ordinary inhabitants of the realm, including clerks but excluding knights and squires, were ordered to pay one hundredth of the value of all their property to the king for the defense of the realm. As far as we know there was no attempt to connect this tax with the principle of universal military service. It was simply a flat demand for payment, and the fact that no attempt was made to hide the newness of the idea shows how strong the government felt at the time. The actual ordinance imposing this tax has not been found, but we know that some of the great nobles were consulted. Thus the duke of Burgundy, in return for consenting to the levy was granted half the proceeds in his lands.[148] An attempt was made to placate other nobles by giving them a share of the money taken from their subjects.[149] Yet there cannot have been a general consultation of the magnates, since the count of Rodez with other nobles of Auvergne protested violently against the tax in August 1295.[150] The order for the tax was probably made by the king with his small group of habitual councillors. The hundredth

[147] Mignon, *op. cit.*, no. 1215, has confused several writers by referring to this tax as the *second* hundredth. But it is evident from his own statements, nos. 1216, 1241, 1244, 1248, that the tax was collected in 1295 and that no other tax of this sort came so early. Two entries, nos. 1295, 1974, indicate that some money was collected before Easter 1295.

[148] E. Boutaric, *La France sous Philippe le Bel*, p. 260.

[149] R. Fawtier, *Comptes du trésor*, p. 21. A.N., K 36B, no. 37, 39, the chapter of Paris gave the king permission to tax their men, June 1295. *Collection de documents inédits, Mélanges historiques*, II, 342, the church of Angers gave its consent to the levy of the hundredth on its lay subjects, 8 February 1296 (n.st.), and stipulated that it was to be collected by delegates of the chapter.

[150] G. Saige, *Documents historiques relatifs à la Vicomté de Carlat* (Monaco, 1900), I, 210, 217.

was collected very promptly, which would seem to indicate that there was no great objection to it. Several final accounts for the levy were turned in before the end of the year in which it had been ordained,[151] an event which is very rare in the case of Philip's later taxes.

The success of the hundredth encouraged the government to reimpose the tax at a higher rate. A few prelates and barons were assembled early in January 1296 and by their advice, as the government was careful to point out, a levy of a fiftieth of the value of all property was ordained.[152] As before, property of nobles was exempted, and in addition men with less than 10 l. were taxed at a lower rate. In an attempt to avoid opposition by the magnates a provision was made granting one third the proceeds of the tax in their lands to counts or bishops and one fourth to other lords with high justice. The government also promised that the tax would not be asked again. Assessments were to be made by three men chosen in each locality, and lords who had high justice supervised collections in their lands.

In spite of the emphasis put on the assent of the magnates to the tax and the obvious attempt of the govern-

151 Mignon, nos. 1241 (Bourges), 1244 (Brittany), 1250 (Cotentin), 1258 (Auvergne).

152 *Ord.*, XII, 333, ". . . cum consilio baronum et prelatorum qui pro ista ordinatio facienda vocati et presentes fuerunt in generali convocatione . . ."; "cum nuper pluribus prelatis, baronibus, et fidelibus regni nostri super arduis ipsuis regni statum tangentibus evocatis presentibus . . . tractatibus et collacionibus congruis prehabitis tandem ad reprimendos . . . inimicorum nostrorum et regni nostri presumptuosos insultas . . . providi deliberacione concilii ordinatum fuit et statutum ut certis subsidiis ab eisdem incolis faciendis. . . ." The actual date of the ordinance is not given but collectors were commissioned 7 January 1296 (n.st.).

ment to be conciliatory there was more opposition to this tax than to the hundredth of 1295. It is not surprising to find protests in Flanders [153] and in the Majorcan part of Montpellier,[154] since these districts were still sensitive to extensions of royal power. But there was open resistance to the collectors in the *bailliage* of Chaumont and the government either could not or dared not punish those who resisted.[155] Collections were slow in the whole *bailliage* of Sens [156] and the tax could be collected in the bishopric of Langres only "per vim et violentiam armorum." [157] The count of Rodez protested again and this time his subjects were freed from paying.[158] The count of Foix also protested and received

[153] F. Funck-Brentano, *Les origines de la guerre de cent ans, Philippe le Bel en Flandre* (Paris, 1896), p. 167, letter of Philip to the count of Flanders on 7 April 1296. The count had not been present at the meeting which ordered the subsidy, but he later agreed to let his subjects pay it provided it were assessed and collected by his authority. Ypres, Bruges, Lille, and Douai negotiated directly with the king and offered him lump sums to avoid assessment of the tax by officials of the count. The king accepted the offer, and, to atone for this breach of his promise to take nothing except through the count's authority, offered the count one-half the proceeds. Thierry de Limburg-Stirum, *Codex Diplomaticus Flandriae* (Bruges, 1879), I, 133, the count of Flanders later protested that the agreement was not kept. *Cf. Ord.*, XI, 380, 381.

[154] B.N., ms. lat. 9192, fol. 66.

[155] Mignon, no. 1327, ". . . rotulus in quo sunt nomina plurium personarum que fecerunt plures recusias a collectoribus qui voluerunt levare dictam quinquagesimam in baillivia calvimontis . . . rex debet habere emendas ab eisdem . . ." —and this was written almost thirty years later!

[156] B.N., ms. lat. 9783, fols. 65, 71, 78, 84, 23, 28, 29, 31v, 41v, large sums from this tax were still being received in the *bailliage* of Sens in 1298 and 1299, and such entries are much more frequent than those for any other district.

[157] Mignon, no. 1292.

[158] B.N., Coll. Doat 156, fol. 78; G. Saige, *Documents historiques relatifs à la Vicomté de Carlat*, I, 223.

at least a temporary respite.[159] Apparently the consent of a small council of nobles friendly to the king had no binding force in the eyes of the great lords of the outlying parts of the country.

The government was quite possibly sincere in 1296 in hoping that there would be no more fiftieths. But in 1297 the count of Flanders allied himself with England and the war became more serious. A new tax was necessary and it seems to have been decided in principal that it was to be another fiftieth. This time, however, the king and the council seem to have made a greater effort to avoid opposition. If the statement of an objector to the tax may be believed they ordered that it should be taken only with the consent of those who paid.[160] The statement is certainly true to this extent, that the collectors were empowered to make any sort of a bargain with the people of their district which would bring in money, and that many groups paid lump sums instead of a fiftieth. Thus the towns of Reims and Chalons refused at first to pay the tax, but eventually fined with the collectors, on what basis we are not told.[161]

[159] *H.L.*, IX, 194; X, col. 335; B.N., Coll. Doat 176, fol. 172. This protest is complicated by the fact that the constable apparently asked for additional aid in men or money from the southern provinces, and that the count was especially grieved by this second request. However the count is respited from giving "exercitum, donum, seu mutuum ratione ipsius exercitus et poenam et quinquagesimalem subsidium," August 1296.

[160] *H.L.*, X, 341, protest of procurator of count of Foix to tax-collector. In trying to force the men of Foix to pay you act "contra ordinationem dicti domini Regis et sui consilii super his factam . . . qui non vult ad predictum subsidium faciendum aliquem compelli invitum, nisi voluntarie et liberaliter sibi placeat subvenire, sicut dictus dominus noster Rex pro pluribus locis hujus senescallie Carcassone vobis scripsit . . . ," 31 May 1297.

[161] B.N., ms. fr. 25992, no. 54, account of Raoul de Meulan and Philippe

Curiously enough the same collectors were sent to the *bailliages* of Caen and the Cotentin and there too they substituted another kind of levy for the property tax.[162] These are the only northern regions for which we have positive evidence that special arrangements were made. But in the South the fiftieth seems to have been generally transformed into other types of taxation. In the *sénéchaussée* of Carcassonne the collector asked at first for a payment of 8 s. from each hearth, but eventually compromised on lump sums which each subdivision of the province promised to pay both in 1297 and 1298. Thus the *viguerie* of Béziers was to pay 12,658 l.t. each year, the *viguerie* of Minervois 2613 l.t., and so on. The total promised was 35,774 l.t. or 71,548 l.t. for the two years.[163] We have one example of the way in which such arrangements were made. The men of the bishop of Albi and of the monastery of St. Salvi of Albi protested against the 8 s. levy to the representatives of the king at Paris, and sent procurators to maintain their case. The procurators finally agreed with the royal agents that the men were to pay a lump sum, equal to the amount which could be raised by a 6 s. hearth-tax, every year that the war lasted. In return they were to be free from all demands for loans, gifts, aids and other exactions.[164] Here is a clear case of local consent to taxa-

---

le Convers, whom Mignon, no. 1203, tells us collected the tax in Chalons and elsewhere. They spent 7 l. 8 s. in notifying the king of the "inobediencia civium de Rem. et Cathal." and 5 l. 2 s. in getting royal approval of a fine arranged with these towns.

162 B.N., ms. fr. 25992, no. 54[2]; Mignon, nos. 1193, 1204.

163 A.N., K 496, no. 3, m. 6.

164 *H.L.*, X, col. 345, ". . . tractatu inter nos, nomine domini Regis et procuratores predictorum super his habito, graviora evitare volentes, in

tion. The fact that the letters embodying this agreement were sent not only to the seneschal of Carcassonne, in whose jurisdiction the men were, but also to the collectors of the fiftieth in Carcassonne, Beaucaire and Rouergue, would indicate that the government expected similar bargains to be made elsewhere in the South. We know that the men of Millau in Rouergue were freed from certain dues in return for consenting to pay the tax.[165] Beaucaire paid a tax assessed on the number of hearths in each district.[166] The fact that Mignon has no record of the collection of the fiftieth in Toulouse and Périgord-Quercy but merely a note that they paid an aid in 1297 indicates that in those districts also there was a shift to the hearth-tax.[167]

In spite of the willingness of the government to bargain with local authorities there were the usual protests against the tax. Large arrears piled up in the North, some of which seem never to have been collected.[168] The magnates of the South were especially bitter, since they had already made larger contributions to the Gascon war than the nobles of the North. Most of them had

---

quantum in eis est consenserunt quod homines predicti dabunt domino Regi singulis annis in subsidium guerre presentis, ipsa guerra durante, illam pecunie quantitatem que esset si a singulis focis VI sol. parvorum Tur. levarentur . . . ita quod, ipsa guerra durante, sint immunes ab omni dono, mutuo, subsidio, et exactione alia. . . ."

[165] M. A. F. de Gaujal, *Études historiques sur le Rouergue* (Paris, 1858–9), II, 140, the town was freed from the "droit de passage et de commun de paix. . . ."

[166] A.N., K 36B, no. 46.

[167] Mignon, nos. 1209–1215, 2391, 2395.

[168] *Ibid.*, no. 1173, 4471 l. "in sufferentia" in Paris; no. 1176, 10284 l. left as arrears in Vermandois; B.N., ms. lat. 9783, fols. 97v, 105v, 106, 109, 10v, payments for this tax were made late in 1299 and 1300.

served in person in the army and the South had paid a local tax for defense in 1294 (and perhaps in 1296) as well as the general subsidies.[169] The town of Narbonne, the prelates and barons of Rouergue, the counts of Foix, Armagnac, Astarac, and Rodez all protested against taxes in 1297.[170] It is doubtful that they obtained much satisfaction that year; at least the county of Foix is listed as one of the regions which agreed to pay lump sums in that year.[171] But the southern taxes were to be collected for at least two years, and there are indications that in 1298 some relief was given to those who had protested.[172]

The government must have had almost enough money for its needs after the collection of the fiftieth of 1297. The Church paid double tenths in 1297 and 1298 and the war with England and Flanders was halted by the truce of Vyve-Saint-Bavon. No subsidies were needed in 1298 or 1299. When the truce expired in 1300 England had deserted Flanders and the French government decided to occupy the county. This was not a difficult

169 *H.L.*, X, col. 345, both a fiftieth and a twenty-fifth were being collected in Beaucaire, Carcassonne and Rouergue. I assume that the latter tax was a special local levy such as had been collected in 1294, and perhaps in 1296, see note 159.

170 *Ibid.*, IX, 201, 202, 206. De Gaujal, II, 140, says that the prelates and barons of Rouergue were given a hearing before the king 21 July and that nothing was collected in their lands before the hearing. The king made no decision but referred the case to Parlement.

171 A.N., K 496, no. 3, m. 6, the county of Foix agrees to pay 4191 l. a year in 1297.

172 *H.L.*, IX, 206, no aid to be taken from count of Rodez if subjects of counts of Foix, Armagnac and Astarac are excused; *ibid.*, 207, the inhabitants of the bourg of Narbonne are to be treated gently in regard to the aid; *ibid.*, X, col. 351, arrears of this subsidy are not to be collected in Toulouse, April 1298 (or 1299).

operation from a military point of view, but it was almost as expensive as a real war. Money was needed again, and a third fiftieth was imposed [173] on the country.

As far as we can tell this was collected much as the earlier fiftieths had been. Lords with high justice supervised the collection in their lands and received a share of the profits.[174] Those who paid were freed from all other charges or services connected with the war.[175] Special arrangements could be made with the collectors whereby other taxes or lump sums could be paid instead of the fiftieth. As in 1297 the North took little advantage of this provision,[176] while most of the southern *sénéchaussées* preferred to arrange other forms of payment. By bargaining with the collectors about the form of the tax they were able to maintain the appear-

[173] *H.L.*, X, col. 388, in the order to Montpellier to pay nothing is said about consent of the magnates. This is a demand for payment of the "ultimi subsidii nuper indicti . . . auctoritate domini nostri Regis. . . ."

[174] B.N., ms. fr. 25992, no. 8, the seneschal of Saintonge accounts for expenses in collecting the fiftieth. In one sergeanty of 715 l. collected the nobles got 145 l. In another the nobles took about 93 l. out of 1036 l. Bib. de Rouen, ms. 33401 (Leber 5870 t. 4), fol. 101, joint account for this tax of royal collector and collector of the bishop of Troyes in the *bailliage* of Vitry. A.N., K 37A, no. 6, a noble in Beaucaire collects the subsidy himself, under supervision of the royal collector, June 1300.

[175] Le Roux de Lincy, *Histoire de l'hôtel de ville de Paris* (Paris, 1846), p. 149, the men of Paris are excused from military service in return for paying the fiftieth; *Olim*, II, 435, men of St. Germain-des-Près are excused from paying an aid to the abbot for his military expenses because they contributed to the fiftieth.

[176] Mignon, nos. 1268–1383; B.N., ms. lat. 9783, fols. 117v, 118v, 120v, the following districts paid a fiftieth in 1300: Paris, Senlis, Vermandois, Sens, Orleans, Bourges, Caux, Caen, Cotentin, Troyes, Vitry, Chaumont, Poitou, Auvergne, Amiens, Touraine, Mâcon, Lyonnais. I give this list because Boutaric once doubted (*La France sous Philippe le Bel*, p. 265) that this levy was general.

ance of paying only of their own free will. Thus the record of the collector for Beaucaire speaks of the aids *granted* the king in place of the fiftieth.[177] In Carcassonne each district, except Béziers, fined with the collector to avoid the fiftieth. In Béziers the non-nobles were trying to make the nobles pay a share of the tax and apparently nothing could be collected until the suit ended.[178] Special arrangements were also made in Périgord-Quercy.[179]

On the whole there is less record of opposition to this fiftieth than any other. It seems fairly certain that all those who had property worth less than 20 l. were exempt; at least this was the limit in districts as widely separated as Paris and Rouergue.[180] It will be remembered that in 1296 all men with more than 10 l.t. had to pay the tax. The increased exemption in 1300 probably meant that the ordinary peasant did not have to pay, and lords who had no subjects except peasants were not annoyed by the presence of royal tax-collectors. Generous exemptions and low assessments may have calmed the opposition. The subjects of the king of Majorca at Montpellier, and of the count of Rodez, who had protested so strongly against earlier taxes, paid this one without much fuss.[181]

177 Mignon, no. 1343 ". . . subsidiis loco quinquagesime in senescallia Bellicadri concessis regi . . ."; but see *ibid.*, no. 1337, "tertia quinquagesima totius ballivie Alvernie concessa regi anno 1300."

178 *Ibid.*, no. 1341; *Olim*, III, 38.

179 Mignon, no. 1338.

180 Le Roux de Lincy, p. 149; G. Saige, *Documents historiques relatifs à la Vicomté de Carlat*, I, 224.

181 *H.L.*, X, cols. 368, 388. Note that Montpellier paid only 3500 l.t., a very small sum in view of its wealth.

Yet the next time a tax was collected it was on an entirely different basis. In spite of all the modifications in favor of the lords the fiftieth was still a very unwelcome manifestation of royal authority. It was a direct demand for a subject's property; an action not very different from theft, by medieval standards. It upset the feudal hierarchy and weakened the lords' control over their men. The chroniclers of the reign are much more bitter over the hundredth and the fiftieth than over the later payments for commutation of military service.[182] The great quarrel with Boniface VIII began in 1301, and for the next few years the government made desperate efforts to keep public opinion on its side. Removal of an unpopular tax would be especially useful in conciliating the nobles and the middle class. It is also possible that the steadily increasing exemptions from the fiftieth may have made the returns from the tax too low for the needs of the government.

The new tax was based on the theory that all subjects could be summoned to defend the realm in case of emergency. Once summoned they would be glad to buy exemption from actual service. This theory had no stronger historical foundation than the earlier claim that all subjects could be taxed for defense.[183] Yet a demand for military service was less shocking to the medieval mind than a demand for money. Those

[182] *H.F.*, XXI, 205, 634, the hundredths and fiftieths were "quasi jugerum novae servitutis genti prius liberae imponendo"; *ibid.*, XX, 577.

[183] P. Guilhiermoz, *Essai sur l'origine de la noblesse en France* (Paris, 1902), pp. 289–299. It is true that the *arrière-ban* was a well-known right of all the great feudal lords, but while the duke of Normandy, for example, could ask service from anyone in Normandy, the king of France could not have done so before he conquered the duchy.

hardened tax-resisters, the men of Montpellier, suggested to their lord that it might be safe for them to obey a summons to serve in the royal army since they were assured that no effort would be made to convert the service into money.[184] However to take money instead of service was an undoubted prerogative of any ruler by 1300. Once the right to demand universal service was admitted the king could raise an army and obtain the money needed to support it by a single act of summons.

This new plan seems to have been tried out on a small scale in the spring of 1302. Money was needed for support of the army of occupation in Flanders and small fines for commutation of military service seem to have been arranged before the Matins of Bruges (18 May 1302) forced a renewal of large-scale military operations. Thus in announcing the new rules for military service in the *bailliage* of Amiens, 12 June 1302, the government conceded that fines arranged earlier in the year protected the payers from service or new fines for a month.[185] Fines collected in Paris in 1302 were returned, perhaps because the town later agreed to pay the large sum of 10,000 l.t. for support of the army.[186]

Whatever the policy before the Matins of Bruges, there is no doubt that a great effort to raise men and money began after news of the disaster reached Paris. The king declared that everyone owed service for defense of the realm and summoned all subjects, includ-

[184] *H.L.*, X, col. 400 ". . . senescallus ipse non intendat convertere dictos pedites armatos in pecuniam . . . ," 16 October 1302.

[185] *Ord.*, I, 345.

[186] Mignon, 1430; Le Roux de Lincy, *Histoire de l'hôtel de ville de Paris*, p. 155.

ing the men of his vassals, to the army.[187] Nobles who were not incapacitated were to serve in person; non-nobles with property of any sort worth 200 l. or chattels worth 100 l. had to serve or fine for exemption. At least one fiftieth of the value of the property was to be paid as a fine and more if the collector could get it. At the same time free consent to fines had to be obtained and collectors were not to use force or threats in obtaining them.[188] The tax was to be based on the individual consent of everyone who paid, secured by negotiations between him and the collector.

The defeat at Courtrai came soon after this levy was ordered. It was a tremendous blow to royal prestige. The pope had predicted that the king's evil advisers would be punished, and his words were justified with startling rapidity. The slaughter at Courtrai seemed a judgment of God against the whole royal policy. Naturally it was difficult to obtain men or money in these circumstances. Urgent letters were sent to local officials, 5 August 1302, asking them to rush troops to the front,[189] but by October the government had had to relax its demands. Nobles with less than 40 l. annual income and non-nobles with less than 300 l. in chattels or 500 l. of all goods were exempted from fines. Most important of all, if a noble had served in the army his

[187] *Ord.*, I, 345, 350.

[188] *Ibid.*, I, 350, secret instructions to collectors. Summon all non-nobles to army. "Si vero quia labori suo parcere et penam proprii corporis redimere voluerint et finare vobiscum . . . de gratia speciali concedimus ut ad financiam pro qua finare vobiscum de ipsorum assensu voluerint non coacti recipiatis eosdem." 7 July 1302.

[189] *Archives historiques du Poitou*, XIII (1883), doc. no. 189. B.N., ms. lat. 9192, fol. 86, Montpellier, summoned to send men on 9 July, does not even consult its lord about obeying until 16 October.

subjects were not bound to pay for exemption from service.[190] These limitations made it possible to collect the tax. Surprisingly large sums were paid, considering the exemptions. For example the assessment on Périgord-Quercy was 22,991 l.t. and Poitou actually paid 22,660 l.t.[191]

The shock of defeat in 1302 had forced the government to lower its tax-rate, but it could not keep taxes at this level and still support an army large enough to defeat the Flemings. In March 1303 the first steps were taken to get more money. With the advice and consent of certain prelates, barons, and other members of the Council the king imposed a twenty per cent income tax on those who had more than 100 l.t. annual income from land and a two per cent property tax on those who had more than 500 l.t. in chattels.[192] To avoid opposition several important concessions were made. No other subsidy, loan, or service was to be asked from those who paid the tax. No supplies were to be seized for the use of the army except for a just price with immediate payment. This provision soon became very embarrassing, since the government did not have enough ready money to make cash payments. It did not dare violate its promises openly, but local officials were instructed to urge sellers to accept assign-

[190] A.N., JJ 36, no. 28, the collection of money, suspended in the *bailliage* of Mâcon, is to be resumed on these terms, 18 October 1302. *Ord.*, I, 350, collectors of fines in Caen are reminded of the new rules, 9 November 1302.

[191] Mignon, nos. 1457, 1461.

[192] *Ord.*, I, 370, ". . . de fidelium prelatorum, baronum et aliorum consiliariorum nostrorum ad hoc presentium consilio et assensu duximus ordinandum." The printed copy of the ordinance is dated 30 March 1303 (n.st.) but A.N., JJ 36, no. 46, gives a copy sent to certain collectors dated 23 March.

ments on the revenues of their districts instead of cash.[193] Those who paid the tax were also freed from any promise which they had made to furnish sergeants for the army. Apparently after the end of the campaign of 1302 an attempt had been made to plan for 1303 by getting pledges to send soldiers. Finally the promise was made that if the king should restore the coinage to its old fineness no new tax for this purpose would be taken from those who paid the subsidy. This was an important concession, since the landed aristocracy was insistent in its demands for reform of the currency, and it was becoming clear that the operation would soon have to be performed. The clergy, unprotected by this promise, later paid a two-year tenth for reform of the currency.[194]

As before the consent of a small group of royal favorites, even with these concessions, was not enough to impress the country. So instructions were sent to the local collectors ordering them to travel about their districts explaining and justifying the ordinance. The leading men of each town or of several towns were to be assembled and shown how "piteable pour le menu peuple et courtoise à ceus qui payeront" the ordinance was; how much less burdensome a money payment was than military service. If they could be put in the proper frame of mind they would be much more generous in

[193] A.N., JJ 36, no. 73, order to the *bailli* of Rouen. Approach owners of food and supplies "au plus aimablement et en la meillour maniere que vous pourrez et par douces paroles et suasions les menez à ce que lez diz biens et vivres vous puissiez prendre et lever par leur gré et par leur volenté sauf ce qu'il ne puissent dire que vous faciez ce contre la dite ordenance. . . ." Pledge your own credit, that of your friends, and if necessary local revenues to get these supplies. June 1303.

[194] See above, p. 42.

valuing property and income.[195] Here is a clear recognition of the importance of obtaining the community's approval of the taxes which it had to assess.

The level of this first tax was only slightly higher than the revised rate of 1302 and it seems to have caused no immediate protest. Perhaps the fact that the great ordinance for reform of the government was announced at the same time [196] made the tax more bearable. There is no actual proof that the magnates insisted on reform in return for consent to taxation, but the ordinance certainly included articles which the magnates had long been demanding. The growth of royal influence within the lands of great lords was to be checked, royal officials were not to interfere with the administration or courts or other men's land, and all high royal officials were to be chosen by the great council, a body controlled, in theory at least, by the great nobles. There is no evidence that these declarations ever had much effect but they may have seemed impressive at the time.

By May the government felt that it could risk the next step. The *arrière-ban* was proclaimed and all men capable of bearing arms were summoned to Arras.[197] At

[195] *Ord.*, I, 370, "car il seront deportez et quittes de l'ost de cette saison et des sergens . . . et de toute autre subvention . . . les quelles choses leur peussent estre assez plus grieves . . . pourquoi il doient plus tost et plus volentiers et plus largement estimer ses biens. . . ."

[196] *Ibid.*, I, 357, the ordinance for reform is dated 18 March 1303 (n.st.), only five days before the request for the subvention.

[197] *Ord.*, I, 546, all those who did not fine according to the earlier ordinance are expected to serve in the army, 18 May. A.N., JJ 36, no. 85, letters to all the *baillis* and the seneschals of Saintonge and Poitou. Everyone is bound to aid in defense, "tant par nature et par droit de pais comme par vertu de riere ban le quel nous entendons orendroit avoir leu et auquel nul ne puet . . . soi escuser que il ne doit obeir. . . ." June.

the same time new instructions were sent the collectors. Nobles of military age with 50 l. annual income had to serve or pay an income tax of fifty per cent. This was reduced to twenty-five per cent for women, children, and invalids who held fiefs. Non-nobles with 20 to 100 l. income from land or 50 to 500 l. in chattels, who had been exempt from the first tax, now had to pay ten per cent of their income and two per cent of the value of their personal property [198] if they wished to avoid service. The collectors were again ordered to explain to the people how necessary the tax was and how moderate were the king's demands. They were secretly warned against going to extremes, especially with the nobles. If necessary they might accept fines from the nobles at a lower rate than that set by the government. Moreover they were to collect no money in the lands of a baron against his will. If they could not obtain the consent of a baron by "bonnes manières" and "belles paroles" they were to send his name to the government which would consider the matter.[199]

It is evident that there was some uneasiness about imposing the new tax on the country. This is understandable since the number of people who had to pay was greatly increased, and each region had to make larger payments. In the one district where the results are known the second tax brought in more money than the first.[200] By decreasing the exemptions the government had doubled the total amount of money

[198] *Ord.*, I, 546, 371.

[199] *Ibid.*, 371.

[200] B.N., ms. n. a. fr. 20025, nos. 52–57. The first tax yielded 3910 l.t. in the *bailliage* of Caen, the second 4801 l.t.

it was taking from the country. Naturally the barons might object to this increase in demands on their subjects.

The two taxes, the greater and lesser subvention, as they were called, were collected throughout the country.[201] Even in the South there seems to have been more uniformity than usual, although there the rates for the second tax were not fixed and more was left to the discretion of the collectors.[202] Judging from the fragmentary reports in Mignon, the collectors had little trouble in the North and West, but met opposition in the Center and South. Thus while Touraine paid 17,111 l.t. of an assessment of 17,701 l.t., Sens paid only 12,650 l.t. out of 19,599 l.t. Bourges had an even worse record with payments of 10,564 l.t. on an assessment of 25,095 l.t. There were large arrears in Orleans and Auvergne as well.[203] In Toulouse the attempt to collect the subsidy was abandoned by 17 August 1303, and fines for disobedience were remitted![204]

Opposition to taxation in 1303 was no more acute than it had been earlier, and apparently the government was not deterred by troubles in certain districts. It was

[201] Mignon, nos. 1429, 1467, 1468, 1473, 1483, 1497, 1504, 1506; A.N., J 241A; both taxes are mentioned in the accounts of Paris, Senlis, Orleans, Touraine, Cotentin, Poitou, Auvergne, and Brittany.

[202] *Ord.*, I, 369, the first tax was imposed in Toulouse, Rouergue, and the Agennais. *H.L.*, X, col. 413, in Beaucaire at the time of the second tax the collectors were to impose a "subvencionem pro servicio nobis in exercitu predicto ab eorum singulis debito juxta facultates cujuslibet. . ." but individual fines for exemption from the subsidy could be arranged. A. Baudouin, *Lettres inédites de Philippe le Bel* (Paris, 1887), no. 175, in Toulouse a certain number of sergeants were to be paid for.

[203] Mignon, nos. 1483, 1484, 1472, 1478, 1475, 1506.

[204] Baudouin, no. 176.

desperately anxious to win a decisive victory and in June it made a new appeal for aid. It could not ask for money but it did suggest that all able-bodied men, even those who had paid the subvention, should join the army.[205] Only moral suasion was to be used, but even this seems to be contrary to the spirit, if not the letter, of the earlier ordinances. The government must have felt very sure of itself, or very desperate, to ask for service from men who had just paid for exemption.

The campaign of 1303 accomplished nothing, and by fall the government was already planning for the next year's expedition. A small council, composed of three bishops, the king's two brothers, Gaucher de Chatillon and Béraud de Mercoeur commanders of the royal army, and four other magnates equally devoted to the king met about 5 October. At this meeting it was decided to ask the nobles to furnish one fully-equipped horseman, for each 500 l. of income from their lands, while non-nobles were to support six sergeants for each group of a hundred hearths. In return the king promised to ask no other aid or service during 1304 and to pay immediately at a price agreeable to the owner for all provisions taken for the use of the army. (This last promise was broken even more flagrantly than it had been in 1303; by June the government was pledging local revenues instead of paying cash and authorizing its agents to seize food by royal authority even when the owners were unwilling to sell.)[206] Moreover, at the

[205] A.N., JJ 36, no. 85. There is to be no constraint, but appeals are to be made to "la reverance que il ont eue touz jours à l'amour du pais et du roiaume."

[206] *Ibid.*, no. 74.

request of the prelates and barons present at the council, the king promised to reform the currency and recall debased money by All Saints' 1304.[207] This was a very important concession to the magnates, who had suffered severely from the depreciation of the currency. Much of their income came from rents and payments in place of services, which had been fixed once and for all in the comparatively stable period of the twelfth and thirteenth centuries. Now they were being paid in coins which were worth only about one-third their face value, while the price of everything which they bought was increasing. Return to the old coinage would double the real income of many nobles. For the government reform of the currency was a serious matter. A large part of the expense of the war had been met by the profits of inflation.[208] Deflation would not only cut off this revenue, but would probably jar the economic life of the country so that all other revenues would decrease. There must have been desperate need for money or great pressure from the magnates to induce the government to make this promise.

As usual the consent of the council, even when accompanied by important concessions, was not enough; the rest of the country had to be convinced, too. This was especially true when consent had been given by such a hand-picked group as that which met on 5 October 1303. Even the government felt that it had to apologize for the composition of the council. It explained that there was no time to summon other magnates, because the emergency was too great to permit

[207] *Ord.*, I, 383 (the fullest form), 408 (gives names of members of council).

[208] Borrelli de Serres, II, 444–447.

delay;[209] a rather thin excuse since the army provided for by the ordinance was not to assemble for eight months.

So, after obtaining the formal consent of the council, the weary task of getting the actual consent of every group in the realm was begun. Very little progress seems to have been made in this work during the remainder of the year. The attack on Boniface VIII and his subsequent death must have become known just as letters announcing the new levy were reaching their destination, and there is every reason to suppose that the government did not push its demands during this crucial period. Yet the mere announcement of the ordinance seems to have caused indignation. The Chronicle of St. Denis says that the South was on the edge of rebellion, and that only a visit from the king averted an outbreak.[210] It is true that Philip found it expedient to make a long journey through Languedoc in December 1303 and January 1304, and that during this journey he granted important privileges to the town of Toulouse, and to the inhabitants of the *sénéchaussées* of Toulouse and Carcassonne.[211] Moreover, on 20 January 1304, an important modification of the rules for the levy of 1304 was made. Subjects of nobles were now to furnish only four sergeants per hundred hearths, or, if they were *taillables haut et bas*, two sergeants. Towns which did not wish to furnish ser-

[209] *Ord.*, I, 383, "Euz sur ce deliberation et consueil avuecques nos prelaz et noz barons que nous poons avoir en presentement, pource que nous ne poons pas avoir à ceste deliberation touz noz prelaz et barons du royaume sitost comme la necessité du royaume le requiert."

[210] *H.F.*, XX, 675.

[211] *Ord.*, I, 392–394, 399, 402.

geants could escape by paying 2 s.p. per day for each sergeant owed. Nobles, however, must either furnish their mounted men, or pay 100 l. for every 500 l. of income from land.[212]

As a result of these concessions, Philip could announce on 27 February that a subsidy had been granted him in Toulouse, Périgord-Quercy, Rouergue, Carcassonne, Beaucaire and Auvergne.[213] This grant may have been secured from an assembly of nobles of Languedoc, or by individual negotiations with leading men of the region.[214] The question as to who made the grant is not very important, because their consent was not much more binding than that of the October council. The collectors immediately had to start negotiations with the nobles and bourgeois of each *sénéchaussée*. An assembly of the nobles of Toulouse was held 3 April; the towns and nobles of Carcassonne met separately on 10 April; the meeting of the towns of Beaucaire took place on 16 April. Each of these groups demanded additional concessions. The nobles of Toulouse insisted on having all the provisions of the king's letter of 20 January inserted in their grant. In addition they obtained permission to pay in installments, to cease paying if peace were made, and to have their own estimate of their incomes accepted. If they paid they were not to be sum-

[212] *Ibid.*, 391.

[213] *H.L.*, X, col. 431, ". . . cum pro negotio guerre nostre Flandrensis iis novissimis diebus quoddam in Tolosana, Caturcensi, Petragoricensi, Ruthenensi, Carcassonne et Bellicadri senescallis ac in ballivia Alvernie subsidium sit concessum."

[214] Dognon, *Histoire des institutions politiques et administratives de Languedoc* (Toulouse, 1896), p. 205, doubts that any general assembly for Languedoc was held at this time.

moned to the army under any pretext. If they went to the army they were to be free from suits for debt. Most important of all, enough money from the grant was to be retained at Toulouse to pay at least half the debts owed the nobles by the king for earlier service in the army.[215] The towns of Carcassonne agreed to send six sergeants or 120 l.t. for every hundred hearths, on condition that their estimate of the number of hearths would be accepted, that collections ceased if peace were made, and that no other service, money or supplies were to be taken from them for a year.[216] The towns of Beaucaire made a better bargain. They received all the assurances given the towns of Carcassonne and in addition were allowed to subtract debts owed by the king to communes or individuals from payments for the subsidy.[217] Since payments for service in the army were always in arrears this provision, if it were observed in good faith, must have reduced the income from the tax considerably. It was not, however, as dangerous a concession in Beaucaire, where forced loans had not been very large, as it would have been in the North.

Even when consent had been obtained from local assemblies the collection of the tax was not assured. Individual towns or lords could still make special bargains with the collectors, and in the process the tax rate was reduced still farther. Thus the town of Carcassonne gave 1000 l.t. for 1273 *feus taillables,* instead of 1530 l.t. which it should have paid if the official rate had been maintained. Béziers did even better, paying only 1848

215 *H.L.*, X, col. 432.

216 *Ibid.*, col. 434. The towns of Toulouse received the same concessions.

217 Ménard, *Histoire de Nismes,* I, *preuves,* 148.

l.t. for 3619 *feus taillables.* The subjects of the count of Foix, the marshal of Mirepoix, and other lords also fined for lump sums.[218] In spite of all these opportunities for bargaining some nobles still refused to allow collection of the tax in their lands. The king had to write a very humble and persuasive letter on 20 June 1304 to the count of Comminges, Gaston d'Armagnac and Ernaud d'Espagne, begging them to allow collection of the subsidy in their lands. They were asked not to set a bad example to their neighbors, and they were promised, as an incentive to induce payment, that they could use the money to pay the wages of the men sent to the royal army to fulfill their feudal obligations.[219]

In the Center and North, as in the South, the government felt the need of securing local consent to taxation during 1304. The nobles of Auvergne secured two charters, one in March and one in May, guaranteeing their rights of justice and protecting their fiefs against sale to pay debts.[220] It seems probable that these charters were granted in return for consent to the tax, especially since the second one acknowledges that their consent to the last subvention was "de pure grace" and was not to bind them in the future. Regional and local assemblies were held in the North. Representatives of the nobles of Normandy were summoned to be at St. Germain-en-Laye on 16 April to discuss the aid for the war, and the nobles of Champagne were ordered to attend a similar meeting at Lagny on 19 April.[221] The letters of summons say that similar meetings have

[218] *H.L.*, IX, 268. [219] *Ibid.*, X, col. 436. [220] *Ord.*, I, 405, 410.

[221] Appendix III. A less complete summons is printed in *H.F.*, XXIII, 795–796.

already been held elsewhere. These meetings were probably called because local authorities had been unable to get the nobles to allow collection of the tax in their lands. We know that many Norman nobles were refusing to allow their subjects to pay in March 1304, and that the government had to restrain overzealous subordinates who wanted to collect the tax without waiting for consent.[222] Apparently the Norman meeting was not an immediate success, though the government tried to point out to the nobles that they could not be paid for their military services unless a tax were collected. A later, undated letter says the nobles of Normandy are still refusing to allow collection of the tax asked by the king and that therefore they are not to be allowed to take an aid from their men to pay their expenses in the army.[223] In the end some sort of arrangement must have been made, since the taxes paid by the Norman *bailliages* in 1304 do not seem abnormally low, and Norman nobles who failed to go to the army dutifully gave the king the twenty per cent of their income

[222] A.N., JJ 36, no. 118, order to all Norman *baillis* to stop taking subsidy "in terris nobilium qui nobis dictam subventionem nondum promiserunt ne in illius prestacione suum prebuerunt assensum." 25 March 1304 (n.st.).

[223] *Ibid.*, no. 208. "Cum nos . . . barones, milites, ceterosque nobiles ducatus nostri Normannie fecissimus requiri ut nobis concederent et donarent . . . subventionem quam ceteri nobiles aliarum partium regni nostri nobis . . . concessisse noscuntur, videlicet de singulis quingentis libratis terre centum libras, ipsique recusaverint in hac parte annuere votis nostris, et nichilominus a subditis suis subventionem ratione exercitus . . . exigere et legare nitantur . . . mandamus tibi . . . quatinus non permittas quod dicti nobiles, vel alter eorum, a subditis suis exigant seu levent subventionem quamcumque ratione exercitus. . . ." This letter is published by Funck-Brentano, *Philippe le Bel en Flandre*, p. 461, with the erroneous date of 1303. As the quotation shows, the letter refers clearly to the rate of the 1304 subvention, and is associated in the register with documents of that year.

which he had asked.[224] It is possible that local meetings of the nobles of each *bailliage* were held, and that in this way their assent to the plan of taxation was secured. We know that such assemblies were provided for the towns of Normandy, since we have a record of the meeting of the representatives of the towns of the *bailliage* of Rouen on 1 May 1304. Charles of Valois, who had been sent by the king to secure the consent of the towns to a subsidy, presided at this meeting. The bourgeois agreed to give six sergeants per hundred hearths, or 2 s. per sergeant per day, but imposed conditions very like those which the townsmen of the South had secured. The statement of local authorities as to the number of hearths was to be accepted and the royal government was not to try to increase the figure by sending in outside investigators. If the towns chose to support a contingent of sergeants they were to be paid directly by agents of the townsmen, and not through agents of the king. The aid was to stop if peace or truce were made. There were to be no other charges or demands for service during the year. Supplies for the army could be taken only with cash payment, and the king was to reform the currency by November.[225]

Besides these meetings with groups of nobles and bourgeois there must have been negotiations with individuals. Thus the archbishop and other prelates of the province of Reims were asked for only one sergeant per hundred hearths. The lands of the queen mother

224 B.N., ms. fr. 9501, fols. 73–75v, extracts by Du Cange from a roll giving names and amounts paid by nobles in the viscounties of Rouen, Orbec, Pont de l'Arche, and Auge. About one hundred paid in each viscounty and few of them were women or minors.

225 Boutaric, *Notices et Extraits*, XX, pt. 2, no. 21.

also benefited by this reduced rate.[226] The lands of the count of Dreux, the count of Anjou, and other Northern nobles had to send four sergeants per hundred hearths, which was normal, but serfs on these lands were entirely exempted.[227] Elsewhere, it will be remembered, serfs had to send two sergeants per hundred fires. The lands of the countess of Montfort paid the tax only in 1305, which would again indicate a special agreement.[228] Many towns in Saintonge and Poitou fined for lump sums.[229]

The long and complicated process by which consent to taxation was secured in 1304 is simply a fuller development of earlier practices. Resistance to taxation of lay property reached a peak in 1304, as had resistance to taxation of clerical incomes. More precautions had to be taken; more concessions had to be made. Assent of the king's council, even when accompanied by liberal concessions was not enough. Consent of regional assemblies, even if more concessions were granted, was not enough. Consent of local assemblies still had to be secured and they imposed new conditions. Even then important individuals and communities held out and had to be placated by further concessions. Money could not be raised in a hurry and at every stage in the process of obtaining consent the potential revenue from the tax was decreased. It is not surprising that in the years immediately following 1304 the government showed a certain fondness for less complicated operations, such as robbing the Jews and the Templars.

The levy of 1304 probably brought in more money

226 A.N., JJ 36, nos. 159, 160.

227 *Ord.*, I, 413.

228 Mignon, no. 1515.

229 B.N., ms. fr. 20853, fols. 12v, 13.

than any of its predecessors. If the records of individual *bailliages* in 1304 are compared with those of 1303 important increases can be noted. Thus Bourges was assessed at 25,095 l.t. in 1303, of which only 10,564 l.t. were collected, while in 1304 it was assessed at 43,758 l.t. and paid 40,000 l.t.[230] Touraine was assessed at 17,700 l.t. in 1303 and at 45,896 l.t. in 1304. Even if we suppose that the 1303 figure includes only payments from non-nobles we find that the non-nobles in 1304 paid 26,017 l.t.[231] Caen paid 8711 l.t. in 1303 and 22,925 l.t. in 1304.[232] Poitou was assessed at 25,833 l.t. in 1302, paid 24,186 l.t. in 1303, and was assessed at 39,459 l.t. in 1304.[233] It is only fair to add that in other districts, such as Sens and Saintonge there is no such increase in returns.[234]

In the case of the tax of 1304 we can permit ourselves the luxury of a guess at the total sum which it produced. A summary made for the *chambre des comptes* a few years later gives a total of 565,170 l.t. in debased currency.[235] This summary is very incomplete. The man who made it had no figures on Paris, Meaux, Troyes, Senlis, Mâcon, Carcassonne and Rouergue, his figure for Beaucaire is useless, and he substituted the returns of an earlier year in the case of Caux. In some districts he probably neglected to include the amount paid by the nobles, which was accounted for separately.

[230] *H.F.*, XXI, 564; Mignon, no. 1478.

[231] *H.F.*, XXI, 564; Mignon, no. 1483.

[232] *H.F.*, XXI, 565; B.N., ms. n. a. fr. 20025, nos. 52–57.

[233] Mignon, nos. 1457, 1504, 1540.

[234] *H.F.*, XXI, 564, 566; Mignon, nos. 1472, 1461.

[235] *H.F.*, XXI, 564–566. A slightly different version may be found in B.N., ms. fr. 20853, fols. 11v–14.

Fortunately some of these errors and omissions can be corrected. We know that Carcassonne paid 59,465 l.t.,[236] that Beaucaire paid at least 15,821 l.t.[237] more than he allowed, and that his figure for Caux was 16,667 l.t. too low.[238] At least 10,093 l.t. more was paid in Périgord-Quercy than he records.[239] The accounts of Mâcon list 2857 l.t. from the tax at Ascension 1305, and it does not seem unreasonable to assume that at least three times as much had been paid already, making the total from that *bailliage* about 11,000 l.t.[240] Paris paid about 27,250 l.t. in 1303 [241] and must have given at least as much in 1304. There are no figures on which to base a guess as to the amounts collected in Senlis, Meaux, Troyes and Rouergue, but if we assume a total of 30,000 l.t. we are probably not overestimating. This would indicate a grand total of 735,000 l.t. in debased currency. This figure is probably not very accurate, though if anything, it is too low. Its one value is relative; it shows the great importance of the subsidy for defense of the realm. No other tax, not even a clerical tenth, could produce that much money in a year.

The large sums collected in 1304 indicate that the government, by timely concessions, had succeeded in obtaining the effective consent of the country to the

[236] Mignon, no. 2058. The date given is 1294 but from the names of the collectors it is clear that this is a slip and that the reference is to the tax of 1304.

[237] A.N., K 1176, no. 16, by 26 August 1305 collectors had received 22,123 l.t. in Beaucaire.

[238] Mignon, no. 1532, total in Caux, less expenses, 29,239 l.t.

[239] *Ibid.*, no. 1548.

[240] B.N., Coll. Baluze 394, fol. 34. In the same account is a receipt of 10,435 l.t. from Bourges, whose total payments we know were 40,000 l.t.

[241] Mignon, no. 1429.

tax. The fact that Mignon found few deficits in the accounts of this levy also suggests that the tax-payers were satisfied with the agreements which they had made. Yet there were delays in payment and some resistance. The *baillis* and seneschals were repeatedly ordered to hurry up collections.[242] Officials in Normandy were even threatened with corporal punishment for their slowness,[243] which was rather unfair since the nobles of the duchy had been very unwilling to consent to the tax and were probably still sulking. Pressure was put on nobles who were unwilling to pay by summoning them to the army on 12 May.[244] This order was reiterated and broadened on 22 July when all subjects who had not paid for exemption, except the very poor, were summoned to the army.[245] Two cases of violent opposition to tax-collectors are reported in the *Olim*, one in Rouergue and one in Forez.[246] But the greatest resistance seems to have come from the clergy. Since most of them were paying a double tenth to the king in 1304 it is not surprising that they resented an additional tax on their lay subjects. Moreover they had been promised that no tax would be taken from their serfs and we have seen that in Reims this promise was broken. On 28 October the *baillis* and seneschals were told that since the clergy had failed to give aid

[242] A.N., JJ 36, nos. 125, 164 (15 and 18 April); *Archives historiques du Poitou*, XIII (1883), nos. 196, 198 (29 June, 1 July).

[243] A.N., JJ 36, no. 184.

[244] *Ibid.*, no. 146.

[245] *Archives historiques du Poitou*, XIII, no. 199. Note that this order says that the *arrière-ban* has been proclaimed.

[246] *Olim*, III, 260, men of Nant are fined 540 l.t. for rescuing goods seized by tax-collectors. *Ibid.*, 362, men of Montbrison fined 5000 l.t. for driving collectors sent by the *bailli* of Mâcon out of town.

when the *arrière-ban* was proclaimed their temporalities were to be taken into the king's hand until further notice. The clergy of the province of Narbonne were exempted from this order, perhaps because their privilege of February 1304 had not exempted their serfs and therefore they had no grounds for opposing the tax.[247]

The battle of Mons-en-Pévèle, 18 August 1304, while not an overwhelming victory for the French, was enough of a success to wipe out the humiliation of Courtrai and to induce the Flemings to discuss terms of peace. But the treaty which ended the war was not proclaimed until June 1305, and in the interval the French government had to be ready to renew the conflict if negotiations broke down. Therefore an attempt was made to raise money for support of the army in 1305. Out best evidence for this tax comes from Languedoc and it cannot be shown that it was imposed in the North.[248] Perhaps the Southern assemblies had agreed to pay a tax for the duration of the war, as they had in 1297. Since there was no actual fighting in 1305 the new tax was bitterly resented and very little was collected. The towns of Foix shut their gates in the face of the tax-collectors in 1305, though Foix had sent its contingent to the army without protest in 1304.[249] About 13,464 l.t. were collected in Carcassonne in 1305,[250] much less than

[247] A.N., JJ 36, no. 193; *cf. Ord.*, I, 403.

[248] *Archives historiques du Poitou*, XLIV, p. 286, a royal letter of 26 June 1305 orders a tax-collector to allow the town officers of Poitiers to assess and collect the "present" subsidy in their town. However, this might refer to a dispute which had begun in 1304.

[249] *H.L.*, IX, 283. *H.F.*, XXIII, 792, the count of Foix sent eighty mounted men and one thousand sergeants in 1304.

[250] Mignon, no. 2059. A.N., K 1176, no. 16, money was collected in Beaucaire in 1305.

the 59,465 l.t. of 1304. Unless the country was actually at war it was almost impossible to collect a general tax.

The government seems to have decided that it was unwise to try to raise any large sums by general taxation during the years immediately following the peace with Flanders. Even the Church was not asked for grants between 1304 and 1307. It was safer to confiscate the property of Jews and Templars than to tax the whole nation. But in 1308 the king's eldest daughter married Edward II of England, and the government seized on this as an excuse for a general tax. No one could deny that all royal vassals, who had not been specifically exempted, owed an aid on this occasion. But the government tried to extend the aid to the whole country by denying the existence of most of the exemptions, and by collecting the tax from subjects of nobles and prelates as well as from the king's own vassals. These actions naturally caused a storm of protests. Parlement, however, decided that the king could take the aid from all inhabitants of Normandy,[251] and the practice authorized by this ruling was enforced in administrative orders to other parts of the country.[252] A face-saving device, adopted in 1309 in Normandy, and perhaps elsewhere, may have soothed some of the nobles. When a noble paid an aid to the king he always took an aid from his own men and pocketed the difference. Now he was to collect the aid from his men, as before, but was to pass on the whole sum to the king, as a

[251] *Ord.*, I, 453, ruling against Norman laymen, 6 September 1308. *Olim*, II, 502, ruling against Norman clergy, 21 March 1310 (n.st.).

[252] *Ord.*, XI, 423, order to *bailli* of Orleans to take the aid from subjects of the barons; *Olim*, II, 514, the aid was collected from men of St. Denis in the *bailliage* of Senlis.

special favor.[253] This scheme avoided the appearance of direct royal taxation of rear-vassals, though the results were much the same as if they had paid the aid directly to the king.

Most of the towns either claimed exemptions from aids or held that the sums assessed on them were too high. As usual the government was ready to negotiate and to surrender all theoretical claims provided it got the money. Thus Rouen denied that it owed the aid, but expressed its willingness to buy back the customs of the bridge of Rouen and the monopoly of navigation of the lower Seine which it had forfeited in 1292. The government left the question of its right to the aid undecided, and sold the desired privileges to the town for 30,000 l.t. plus the cancellation of a 12,500 l.t. debt owed by the king to Rouen.[254] At the other end of the country, Carcassonne denied owing the aid, but agreed to give the king 2000 l.t. as a gift, and in return obtained confirmation of a tax-farming arrangement.[255] St. Quentin objected to its assessment of 3200 l.p. for the aid, and refused to pay at all. When property of leading merchants was seized in 1310 they grudgingly paid 2000 l.p. and demanded an investigation as to their liability to pay the rest. Apparently nothing more was paid.[256]

The most interesting feature of this tax was the use of Parlement as a place in which consent of tax-payers

[253] A.N., JJ 41, no. 127; Boutaric, "Documents inédits," *Notices et extraits*, XX, pt. 2, no. 38, same ruling in county of Alençon.

[254] A.N., J 392, no. 24.

[255] *H.L.*, X, col. 473.

[256] E. Lemaire, *Archives anciennes de la ville de Saint Quentin*, nos. 220, 221, 222, 224, 231.

could be secured. A form-letter to all *baillis* in 1310 ordered them to try to make some sort of a compromise with subjects of the prelates who refused to pay the aid. If this failed they were to be ordered to send procurators to the next Parlement to "oir et d'acomplir ce que nostre court en ordenera, et le plus sagement et cautement que vous pourrez faites et pourchassiez que leurs diz procureurs aient plain et general povair de greer, acorder, et acomplir ce que noz genz voudront ordener et acorder amiablement avec euls de ceste chose. . . ." [257] This is something more than an ordinary summons to court. The procurators are to act as representatives with power to agree to a tax. Parlement is not going to give a legal decision; it is going to negotiate with these representatives. If this practice had become common, the French Parlement might have become more like the English Parliament, which was also originally a court.

We know that not only subjects of the prelates, but many towns of Quercy and Saintonge sent such representatives to Paris.[258] Many of the procurators represented several neighboring communities. One man acted for eight towns, two men together for twelve towns, one man for three towns and an abbot, etc.[259] Apparently they were talked into making generous grants since Poitou and Saintonge paid 19,053 l.t. for this aid, almost half of what they had paid for the very heavy tax of 1304.[260]

[257] *Olim*, II, 508.

[258] A.N., J 356, nos. 1–14; JJ 42A, no. 72; Ch. V. Langlois, "Les papiers de Guillaume de Nogaret," *Notices et extraits*, XXXIX, no. 186.

[259] A.N., J 356, no. 14.

[260] Mignon, no. 1575; *H.F.*, XXI, 566, Poitou and Saintonge together paid 46,000 l.t. in 1304.

These negotiations and law-suits naturally slowed up collection of the aid. Paris agreed to pay a tallage of 10,000 l.p. in 1308 but arguments as to who should contribute to this tallage were still going on in 1311.[261] It was collected in Amiens, Poitou, Saintonge, Mâcon, and Toulouse in 1310.[262] Collection began in Orleans in 1310 but the order to take the aid from subjects of the barons was not given until 6 October 1311.[263] Since there was no war, the government could spend more time in conciliatory and legal procedures. In 1308 there seems to have been less of that pressure on local officials which forced them to use violent means in collecting taxes.

When Louis of Navarre, the future Louis X, was knighted in 1313, there was another attempt to turn the feudal aid, which everyone admitted was due, into a general tax. As in 1308, there were protests from towns which claimed exemption from all aids, and from nobles who claimed that only tenants-in-chief should pay. This time the protests were much more effective, probably because war with Flanders seemed near and a general subsidy for defense was to be requested.[264] The government could not afford to antagonize powerful subjects when it was soon to require their aid. Many towns, including Sens, Lorris, Poitiers, Niort, and La

[261] Le Roux de Lincy, *Histoire de l'hôtel de ville de Paris*, p. 171; *Olim*, II, 515, 589.

[262] Mignon, nos. 1558, 1575; *H.L.*, IX, 341; Borrelli de Serres, II, 514.

[263] *Ord.*, XI, 423.

[264] See note 269 regarding a subsidy for defense asked before 1 August 1313. A. Longnon, *Documents relatifs au comté de Champagne*, III, 135, 138, 139, the aid for knighting Louis was collected in Champagne from July 1313 to September 1314. *Ord.*, XI, 428, a general subsidy for defense was asked 6 August 1314.

Rochelle were put "en souffrance," that is, no immediate attempt was to be made to collect the aid from them.[265] Subjects of lords with high justice obtained similar respites, and money collected from them was returned.[266] Even with these concessions a small army of sergeants had to be hired to force people to pay in Champagne, and Paris had paid little more than half of its assessment by the end of 1315.[267]

The government had to be conciliatory in collecting the aid of 1313 because both in 1313 and 1314 it planned to raise a general subsidy for support of the army. Flanders had not fulfilled the terms of the treaty of 1305, in spite of endless negotiations. A new conference was held in 1313 and this time the French army was called out to back up the diplomats. There was no fighting, since the Flemings promised once more to observe the treaty, but it was natural that the government should have asked for money when the army was summoned. According to Geoffroi de Paris a general subsidy was imposed, but when peace was assured the king ordered all money taken to be returned.[268] Orders to collectors, dated 1 and 16 August 1313, tell them to collect no more money but say nothing about the disposition of any sums which they may have already received.[269] The expense account of a collector in

[265] J. Petit, *Essai de restitution des . . . mémoriaux de la Chambre des Comptes*, pp. 128–132.

[266] *Ibid.*, p. 128. Longnon, III, 138, 140, 141, examples of communities in Champagne exempted because they were in the lands of lords with high justice.

[267] Longnon, III, 136, 138, 139, 140. B.N., ms. Clairembault 228, p. 948.

[268] *H.F.*, XXII, 140.

[269] Ménard, *Histoire de Nismes*, II, *preuves*, 12; *Archives historiques du Poitou*, XLIV (1923), p. 321.

Toulouse shows that he received only a few hundred pounds and that, while this money was deposited with the receiver of the *sénéchaussée,* it apparently never reached the royal treasury.[270] Mignon found no records of this subsidy, so it appears that Geoffroi was probably right and that little, if anything, was kept by the government.[271]

Flanders observed the agreement of 1313 no better than earlier ones. An open break between the king and the count came early in 1314, and by the middle of the summer it was evident that a new campaign was necessary. The government seems to have been very short of money and a general tax could not be avoided. It was necessary to receive the earlier expedient of summoning all men to the army and then taking fines for exemption. The first step, that of calling out the *arrière-ban,* was taken on 25 July.[272] According to precedent this should have been followed by negotiations with local assemblies and individuals. Instead the government decided to begin work with a great meeting at Paris, at which the needs of the country could be explained and favorable public opinion created. This had been the policy in dealing with the delicate questions of

[270] B.N., ms. fr. 23,256, fols. 39–40, expense account of Jean Guillot, canon of Beauvais, sent to collect subvention in Toulouse in July 1313; "De subvencione levavimus 471 l. 12 s. 6 d. tur. quas recepit dictus thesaurius [of Toulouse] et nichil plus levavimus quia habuimus preceptum de cessando." A corrector has added: "Sciatur ubi dicte 4[71 l.] redduntur regi."

[271] Mignon, no. 1612. "Quedam subventio fuit ordinata levari pro eodem exercitu [Flandrie], anno 1313. . . . Sciatur si fuit levata, quia nullus videtur computasse." Ménard, *Histoire de Nismes,* II, *preuves,* p. 17, the consuls of Nîmes assert in 1314 that the king ordered all money collected in 1313 to be returned because peace was made.

[272] B.N., ms. fr. 16,600, fol. 53. I owe this reference to Professor Taylor.

the attack on Boniface, and the arrest of the Templars. Now it was to be applied, for the first time, to taxation. The government was probably aware that resentment over its earlier exactions still lingered, and that it was going to be difficult to collect a new tax. A solemn assembly, in the king's presence, was an excellent means of spreading propaganda which would check the opposition. Moreover if leading men from all parts of the country could be convinced of the necessity of taxation local collections might proceed more rapidly. These seem to be the basic ideas which led to the summoning of a great assembly at Paris on 1 August.[273] Certainly the meeting had no constitutional significance, since the machinery which would produce the tax had already been set in motion. And, as we shall see, in the arguments over collecting the tax, the decisions of the assembly were not invoked by either side.

The assembly seems to have been limited to bourgeois representing each cathedral city. On 1 August they were brought before the king and a council which included "pluseurs barons et evesques." Enguerrand de Marigny, the king's chief minister, made an able and effective speech. The king's just grievances against the Flemings were recounted in detail. Then Enguerrand asked the town representatives if they were willing to aid the king in his campaign against Flanders. The king rose in his place, to see who was ready to help him. In these circumstances there was only one possible an-

[273] This explanation of the purpose and work of the assembly of 1314 was suggested to me by Professor C. H. Taylor. The reasons for adopting this interpretation may be found in his study of large assemblies called in connection with subsidy campaigns, *infra*.

swer, and it was given by Etienne Barbete, a leading citizen of Paris. He promised in behalf of all that they would give such aid as was in their power. "After this meeting," says the chronicler to whom we owe the one report of the assembly, "a very evil and grievous subvention was raised by advice of the said Enguerrand." [274]

It seems clear that this assembly did not know the terms of the tax which was to be imposed and that it was merely asked to accept the idea that some sort of tax would be necessary. No one ever argued that its assent bound the rest of the country. In the instructions concerning the subvention the king mentions only the consent of his council, with no reference to the approval of the representatives of the towns.[275] In a later letter he says that he can impose and raise such a subvention as part of his royal power, again with no reference to the assent of the assembly at Paris.[276] This is not surprising, since effective consent to taxation had always been obtained from negotiations with local assemblies or individuals. If consent of the council of magnates did not bind other subjects, how much less consent of a small group of bourgeois. Thus once more we are forced to conclude that the Paris assembly was called merely as a means of spreading royal propaganda.

[274] *H.F.*, XX, 691, Chronicle of St. Denis.

[275] *Ord.*, XI, 428, the request is made "par grant deliberation de nostre conseil pour la deffense et la garde de nostre royaume. . . ." Note that the instructions are dated 6 August, while the assembly met 1 August.

[276] Roucaute et Saché, *Lettres de Philippe le Bel*, no. 93. ". . . nobisque liceat ut intendimus de jure nostro facere fieri et levare subventionem predictam. . . ." Note that the protest of the League of Vermandois (quoted below p. 86) makes no reference to assent of an assembly and represents the tax as imposed by royal authority.

Even in this limited sphere it seems to have been rather ineffective.

When the tax-collectors received their instructions it was evident that the government was using the precedents of 1302–04. All subjects were summoned to the army, but those with legitimate excuses could fine for exemption. Fief-holders and those with 2000 l. of any kind of goods had to fine as individuals. All others were grouped in units of 100 hearths, each of which was to send six sergeants, or pay 1 s.p. per sergeant per day plus 30 s. for his equipment. Less might be taken in poor districts. On the other hand in centers of trade a sales-tax might be imposed instead of the hearth-tax, if the collector thought it would bring in more money.[277]

While the basic rate of this tax was lower than that of 1304 the writ contained none of the concessions which had made the earlier levy bearable. No local assemblies were held to allow for the modification of rates or the ventilating of grievances. The government may have hoped that the meeting at Paris would make local assemblies unnecessary. If it did it overestimated, for once, the effectiveness of its propaganda. Neither townsmen nor magnates were enthusiastic about the tax. The situation became worse when peace was made with Flanders in September. On the basis of earlier precedents, it was very doubtful that the king had a right to receive such a tax in time of peace. Yet attempts at collection continued.[278] On 7 October the consuls of Nîmes flatly refused to pay, even after being imprisoned.

[277] *Ord.*, XI, 429.

[278] A. Artonne, *Le mouvement de 1314 et les chartes provinciales* (Paris, 1912), p. 18, continuation of collection of the subsidy is ordered in a letter of 14 October to the *bailli* of Auvergne.

They said that all money collected in 1313 had been returned after peace was made and that the same rule should be applied again.[279] By 28 October the king had had to suspend collection in the lands of the bishop of Toulouse [280] and by 16 November the bishop of Mende and the nobles of the Gévaudan and Rouergue had won similar concessions.[281] Along the eastern frontier the opposition became organized. Leagues of nobles formed in Vermandois, Artois, Champagne, Burgundy and elsewhere protested against the fiscal policy of the whole reign and especially against the last tax. The complaint of the League of Vermandois-Artois gives an especially clear statement of the position of the nobles. "Et encore en cheste année présente courante . . . li dis nostre sires li rois a fait impositions non dehuement seur les nobles et sus le commun du royaume et subventions lesques il s'est efforchiés de lever d'ichaus; la quelle chose nous ne poons souffrir ne soustenir en bonne conscience car ainsinc perdrions nous nos honours et nos franchises et nos libertés et seriemes en servitute à touzjours. . . . Et seur toutes ces choses dessus dites nous avons requis au dessus dit nostre seigneur le roy et à son consaill que drois nous en fust fais. Seur lesquels choses il nous fu respondu que li rois estoit bien

[279] Ménard, *Histoire de Nismes*, II, *preuves*, p. 17, the consuls cannot believe that the king intends "ut aliquid levetur ex dicta financia, set potius eam velit nobis remitti, cum dicta guerra cessavit; quod apparet ex eo quia idem dominus noster rex mandavit restitui quod alias fuit levatum in casu consimili anno preterito, etiam pro guerra Flandrensi, quia illa guerra cessavit."

[280] Baudouin, *Lettres inédites de Philippe le Bel*, no. 121.

[281] Roucaute et Saché, nos. 93, 94. Artonne, *op. cit.*, *pièces justificatives*, II.

enfourmés que ch'estoit ses drois et que autre drois on ne nous en feroit et que li rois estoit assez poissant de contraindre et de punir les rebelles seur ces choses. . . ."[282]

Faced with such opposition, the government had to yield. Just before his death Philip ordered "que ladite subvention cesse du tout."[283] Some overzealous local officials ignored the order, perhaps hoping it would soon be reversed, but apparently all money collected after the tax had been stopped was returned.[284] On the other hand the government seems to have kept all that had been collected before that date. In some districts this amounted to respectable sums. In Carcassonne and Saintonge-Poitou collectors had had time to negotiate with individual communities and the two districts paid respectively 30,165 l.t. and 20,989 l.t. This compares very favorably with the 59,465 l.t., and 46,390 l.t. which they had paid in 1304, since the rate of the earlier tax was higher. Elsewhere, however, the decrease from 1304 is noticeable. Toulouse paid only 17,271 l.t. instead of 73,479 l.t., Orleans 2063 l.t. instead of 23,437 l.t., Vermandois 8967 l.t. instead of 66,319 l.t., and Périgord 2813 l.t. instead of 12,485 l.t. Altogether only

[282] Boutaric, "Documents inédits," *Notices et extraits*, XX, pt. 2, nos. 42, 43. See *H.F.*, XXII, 153, the chronicler Geoffroi de Paris makes taxation one of the chief grievances of the barons in 1314.

[283] *Ord.*, I, 580, Louis X confirms this act of his father's, but does not give its date. It was probably soon after the letter of 16 November (see note 281) in which there still seems to be hope that the tax can be collected, and before 29 November when Philip died.

[284] *H.L.*, X, 556, Louis X orders return of everything collected after receipt of Philip's order suspending the tax; Ménard, *Histoire de Nismes*, II, *preuves*, 19, the imprisoned consuls of Nîmes paid the collectors of the subsidy 400 l.t. as late as 12 December 1314 and began suit to regain it 29 May 1315.

116,516 l.t. were collected in 1314 instead of the 735,000 l.t. of 1304.[285] We may assume that the assessment in 1314 was about half what it was in 1304,[286] and it follows that not more than one-third the amount requested was paid in the country as a whole. The opposition had been very successful in blocking collection until the tax was revoked.

Stopping the subsidy of 1314 had been a great victory, but the leagues of nobles were strangely inept in following up their advantage. Instead of admitting that taxation was inevitable and seeking to control it, as the English baronage had done for at least two generations, they still believed that taxation was unnecessary. Instead of joining with other classes to put effective limits on royal power they were interested above all in preserving their own power over their subjects. They did not insist that the government should secure consent to taxation, but they did insist that their rear-vassals should not be taxed. In view of recent precedents they could not make even this restriction absolute, and as a result the charters obtained in 1315 contain almost no effective limitations on the government's power to tax. The inhabitants of Vermandois were promised only that the last subvention would not be collected. Norman nobles were told that the king would take nothing from their vassals, except when the *arrière-ban* was proclaimed, and that he would order no tallages, exactions,

[285] For all these comparisons see *H.F.*, XXI, 564, 567, except for Carcassonne which may be found in Mignon, no. 2058.

[286] *H.F.*, XXI, 564, 567, Touraine assessed at 45,896 l.t. in 1304 and at 22,259 l.t. in 1314; *ibid.*, 569, Carcassonne assessed at 31,539 l.t. in 1314 while (Mignon, no. 2058) it paid 59,465 l.t. in 1304.

subventions or impositions except in an emergency for the good of the realm. These two exceptions, of course, had been the excuse for every tax since 1295. The nobles of Burgundy-Autun-Langres-Forez were told that no money or service would be asked from rear-vassals "nisi in casu retrobanni in quo casu quilibet de regno nostro tenetur. . . ." This again left the way open for taxes like those of 1304 and 1314. The barons of Champagne won a definite promise that none of their subjects, noble or otherwise, should be asked to pay "l'aide de l'ost," but this would not cover payments asked by virtue of proclamation of the *arrière-ban*.[287] At most, these provisions forbad taxation in time of peace, and could be used to block a levy such as that of 1314. But they contained little to reinforce the idea that consent to taxation must be obtained, and nothing to improve the machinery by which such consent was expressed. When the next general tax was requested Philip V negotiated with local assemblies as his father had done, and on these occasions nobles and townsmen met separately, as they had before.[288] This multiplicity of assemblies handicapped both king and people. The king was injured by delays and resistance in some provinces. The people could never unanimously reject a tax, since some province or class was sure to give in.

In reviewing the history of taxation in the reign of Philip the Fair we find growing resistance but no important constitutional results. By making concessions to local groups, by stopping taxation altogether after periods of stress, the government was able to avoid any

[287] *Ord.*, I, 552, 569, 566, 579–80.

[288] *Ibid.*, I, 677, 692; *H.L.*, X, col. 601.

formal limitations on its power. No pledge, written or implied, bound it to obtain the consent of those paying taxes. Even at the very end of the reign the king could say that he had an unlimited right to take money for the defense of the realm. In practice the government did ask for consent, but it was not bound to obtain that consent in any specified way. It could negotiate with individuals, with towns, with *bailliages*, or with regions such as Languedoc or Normandy. Expediency, not constitutional forms, determined the methods used in obtaining the acceptance of a tax by the country. On the whole the government had gained many useful precedents for future taxation and had lost surprisingly little power in the process.

Yet there had been violent and increasing opposition to taxation. Early in the reign, in 1295, the government was collecting a sales-tax, a heavy forced loan, a tenth from the Church and a hundredth on lay property without much difficulty. By 1303 the first two taxes had almost disappeared, the clergy were asking far-reaching concessions for the grant of a tenth, and the form of the tax on lay property had been completely changed. The demands of local assemblies of clergy and laymen in 1303–1304 forced the government to begin reforming the currency, to pay some of its just debts and to stop encroaching on the jurisdiction of the prelates and barons. It is conceivable that the unfriendly attitude of these assemblies induced the government to make a rather unsatisfactory peace with Flanders in 1305. These were important modifications of policy, but the machinery of government was not changed. The question of taxation was left open, since the king's right to tax was not denied and no permanent checks on that right were devised.

Skillful work by the government prevented serious consequences arising from the opposition of 1303–1304. All taxation ceased for several years. The government met its expenses and diverted the attention of the people by unscrupulous attacks on the Jews and the Templars. The alliance between king and pope soon made clerical resistance to taxation impossible. Laymen were asked only for the lawful feudal aids until 1313.

The attempt to take subsidies for the army in 1313 and 1314 stirred up the opposition again. This opposition may have been responsible for the inconclusive nature of the campaigns of those years since Enguerrand de Marigny, the king's chief minister, was an expert in finance and must have known how dangerous a full-fledged war would be if taxes could not be collected. Opposition to taxation was an important cause of the rise of the leagues of nobles in 1314 but these leagues did not succeed in modifying the form of government. The provincial charters which they gained in 1315 were too full of reservations to be very valuable. The king and the bureaucracy saved most of their powers at the price of a temporary embarrassment. The war had to be abandoned, certain rights of local government were secured to the nobles, but nothing of importance, especially in the field of taxation, was lost.

It has long been recognized that the failure of the French people to secure control of taxation and some voice in legislation was due to the strength of provincial and class feeling. Local assemblies could not control a central government. They were remote from the scene of power and they never adopted a uniform policy. The organization of local assemblies on class lines made it even harder to obtain unity. It has also been claimed that the weakness of central assemblies and the importance of provincial meetings was due to the deliberate policy of the royal government. Except for church councils this does not seem to be true of the reign of Philip the Fair.[289] Multiple negotiations about taxation with individuals and local assemblies were slow and usually resulted in decreasing the amounts paid. Philip IV could not collect a tax as rapidly as Edward I of England and he had to compromise more in matters of rates and methods of payment. The English system of having a tax granted by one body was more efficient, and if the chronicler's story of the meeting of 1314 is accurate the French government was beginning to imitate that efficiency in the last year of the reign. Philip and his officials were not afraid of concentrating representatives of the whole country in one place. Every Parlement brought together men from all the provinces who had grievances against the government. The Estates-General called to support attacks on Boniface and the Templars represented the whole realm. It was not that the government feared central assemblies but that the people were not impressed by them. As we have seen, the consent of a council of prelates and barons to a tax did not bind magnates who were not present. The acquiescence of the council and of town represen-

[289] P. Dognon, *Les institutions politiques*, p. 200, "N'attribuons pas ces consultations séparées à quelque manoeuvre habile des rois ou des sénéchaux: c'était plutôt scruple de leur part et volonté d'obtenir l'agrément de tout le monde."

tatives to the tax of 1314 did not prevent a revolt against that tax. The first attack on Boniface was approved by the Estates-General of 1302, but the more serious charges of 1303 had to be reinforced by the approval of local assemblies and the adhesion of prominent individuals, just as a tax granted by the council had to be confirmed by negotiations with local assemblies and individuals. France was united only in her king and her bureaucracy. No one assembly could speak for France.

Unity was a royal idea in France, not a popular one. Central assemblies were desired by the bureaucracy and not by their opponents. The French nobles of 1300 were still trying to preserve their independence of the royal government. They had not yet learned, as the English barons had learned a century earlier, that their only hope was to unite and gain control of the government. The English barons insisted on their right to be summoned to the king's council, and by dominating the council they could check the king and his household. The French barons grumbled about the composition of the king's council, but they made no move to enlarge it by insisting on summons for all tenants of the crown. The nobles of Rouergue, or Burgundy, or Vermandois could act together, but not the nobles of France.

The bishops seem to have had a clearer idea of the possibility of joint action through the council. The bishop of Viviers insisted on being made a member of the council when he recognized the French king as his sovereign.[290] It will be remembered that the prelates in 1303 asked that all future changes in the currency be

[290] *Gallia Christiana*, XVI, 277.

approved by an assembly of bishops and barons.[291] But without the support of the nobles the council could not become a central assembly for the upper classes, and it remained under the control of the bureaucracy.

The towns, with their insistence on local privileges, were even less likely to ask for central assemblies than the clergy or the nobility. We have seen that they frequently engaged in individual negotiations with tax-collectors even after their representatives had attended provincial assemblies. There is no evidence to show that the towns desired a central assembly.

So the old paradox still holds true. England developed parliamentary government because her early kings were strong. France developed absolutism because her early kings were weak. The strong English kings prevented the formation of provinces and forced the whole country to accept the authority of the central assembly which was part of their government. The French kings were too weak to wipe out provincial boundaries or to create an assembly which was universally respected. They had to govern personally if they were to govern at all, because they could not govern through a Parliament.

[291] Appendix II.

APPENDIX I

List of Tenths and Subsidies Imposed During the Reign of Philip IV

Year	Tenth	Subsidy
1285	Tenth granted by the pope for four years for attack on Aragon.	Aid for knighting Philip the Fair, asked by Philip III, but collected only at the end of 1285 and in 1286.
1286	"	
1287	"	
1288	"	
1289	Tenth granted by the pope for three years for expenses of Aragon war.	
1290	"	
1291	"	
1292		Sales-tax imposed in northern towns, and perhaps throughout realm. Hearth-tax in Saintonge-Poitou to pay for expulsion of Jews.
1293		Sales-tax; Saintonge-Poitou hearth-tax.
1294		Sales-tax; Saintonge-Poitou hearth-tax. Hearth-tax in Languedoc for expenses of occupation of Gascony.
1295	Tenth granted by provincial councils for two years in 1294–5; collected in 1295–6.	Sales-tax; Saintonge-Poitou hearth-tax. Tax of one hundredth on property for expenses of war (military tenants exempt; special arrangements in Languedoc).
1296	"	Sales-tax; Saintonge-Poitou hearth-tax. Tax of one fiftieth on property (military tenants exempt).

Year	Tenth	Subsidy
1297	Double tenth granted by a council at Paris with consent of the pope. (Annates also paid to king this year.)	Sales-tax; Saintonge-Poitou hearth-tax. Tax of one fiftieth on property (hearth-tax or lump sum substituted in many districts).
1298	Double tenth granted by a council at Paris by order of the king. (Annates paid this year.)	Tax of one fiftieth or its equivalent continued in Languedoc.
1299	(Annates paid this year.)	
1300	Tenth granted in 1299 by provincial (?) councils; collected in 1300 and partially in 1301.	Tax of one fiftieth on property worth more than 20 l.t.
1301	Same, collected only for a half-year in Bordeaux and Chartres as result of papal prohibition.	
1302		Fines for exemption from general military service; one fiftieth or more of value of property asked.
1303	Tenth granted by a council at Paris (?), later cancelled in order to induce prelates to pay subsidy.	Fines for exemption from general military service: First subvention — 20% of incomes over 100 l. derived from land, 2% of personal property over 500 l. Second subvention — 10% of incomes between 20 and 100 l. derived from land, 2% of personal property worth 50 to 500 l.
1304	Double tenth from prelates and exempt monasteries, single from other clerics, granted by provincial councils, much of it collected only in 1305–6. (Annates paid this year.)	Commutation of general military service; nobles support one mounted soldier for each 500 l. of income from land; non-nobles support 6 foot-soldiers per hundred hearths or pay hearth-tax.
1305	(Annates paid this year.)	Attempt to continue these taxes in Languedoc.

Year	Tenth	Subsidy
1306	(Annates paid this year.)	
1307	Tenth granted by the pope in 1304 for two years, for restoring the currency, collected in 1307–8.	
1308	"	Aid for marrying the king's daughter (most of it collected only in 1309–11).
1309		
1310	Tenth granted by the pope for one year.	
1311		
1312	Tenth granted by the pope for one year.	
1313	Tenth granted by the pope in 1312 for six years for a crusade; collected 1313–18 (revenue of last year reserved to pope).	Aid for knighting the king's eldest son (much of it collected only in 1314–15). General subsidy ordered, then cancelled when peace with Flanders was made.
1314	"	Fines for exemption from military service. Military tenants and those with property worth more than 2000 l. fine as individuals; all others must support 6 foot-soldiers per hundred hearths. Only one-third of this tax collected.

APPENDIX II

THE DOCUMENT printed below is in the Archives Nationales, carton J 459, no. 22. This carton contains the replies of certain towns consulted by the king in 1314 about plans for stabilizing the currency. Our document was probably placed there because there is a reference to changes in the currency in the last paragraph. This led to a faulty endorsement, "Declaratio prelatorum super facto monete," which does not correspond to the title.

This document is certainly of the reign of Philip IV since it refers to St. Louis as the king's grandfather. It is almost surely of the year 1303. It was written before 1 May 1304 since several of its requests were granted in the ordinance for the Church of that date.[1] It is after Lent 1303, since it refers to the grant of a subsidy made by prelates and barons "in Quadragesima proxima precedenti" and also says that reform of the currency was discussed at the same time. The only grant by the magnates in Lent of which we know was made 30 March 1303 (n.st.) and in this grant the possibility of a reform of the currency is mentioned.[2] A slight difficulty is caused by reference to a reforming ordinance "hoc anno." Philip's great ordinance for reform is dated 18 March 1302 (o.st.),[3] that is, it came just before Easter 1303 and should have been referred to as last year's ordinance by men writing in 1303 and using the French style of dating. However the words "hoc anno" should not be taken too strictly. The government itself in an ordinance dated 30 March 1302 (o.st.) promised to ask no other aid "hoc anno." [4] Since the year officially ended a week after the ordinance was issued the promise was valueless unless "hoc anno" were interpreted as meaning a year from the date of the ordinance. Our prelates, in placing the reforming ordinance in 1303, were probably thinking of the date at which it was received and applied in the provinces. Of course they may have met after 30 March 1303 and before Easter, but their reference to the meeting in March sounds as if it had taken place some time before. As was indicated in the text, the most likely date for this document is June 1303, since we know that the prelates met at that time, and the king refers to a grant by the clergy soon after.[5]

[1] See below, pp. 99 ff.

[2] *Ord.*, I, 369, 370.

[3] *Ibid.*, 357.

[4] *Ibid.*, 370.

[5] See above, p. 34.

The document as we have it is not an official communication to the king. It was never dated or sealed and the names of the prelates who had it written are omitted. It may have been the first draft of a letter to the king, or a memorandum of actions taken at a meeting of the clergy. Yet we know that these proposals reached the king in some form. The document itself says that they were written down at another time by Master Amy (d'Orleans) who was a royal notary. Moreover a great part of the ordinance for the Church of 1304 is based on this document. The fact that it was preserved in the royal archives shows that some government officials considered it important. It may be accepted, then, as an authentic statement of the position of the French bishops in 1303.

Super consilio et auxilio que a nobis prelatis hic presentibus maiestas regia postulavit

Nos prelati predicti, scilicet talis et talis, eidem deliberatione habita respondentes consulimus et rogamus et vobis domino nostro regi quanto instancius possumus supplicamus quatinus iusticiam quam in terris colere summum bonum probatur in regno vestro et in curia vestra faciatis efficaciter observari, in regno vestro instituendo senescallos, baillivos, iudices et alios officiales seu curiales non ex affectione familiarium sed ex industria et legalitate ac prerogativa meritorum officialium eorumdem, assumendo videlicet viros providos et discretos, deum timentes, vestram honorem ac iusticiam plusquam lucrum seu questum pecuniarium diligentes. Circa ipsorum autem officialium correctionem et reformationem intendatur prout per regiam providentiam extitit ordinatum hoc anno.[6] Ipsi quoque officiales ad observandum vestras ordinationes noviter editas, iura, et rationabiles terrarum consuetudines arceantur,[7] sic quod deus et thronus regius honorentur exinde, justicia reddens unicuique

[6] *Ord.*, I, 357 ff. Paragraphs 14–23, 25–34, 38–55 of the ordinance of 18 March 1303 (n.st.) deal with the powers and conduct of royal officials.

[7] *Ibid.*, 407 (ordinance for Church, 1 May 1304), paragraph 7. "Quod ballivi et alii officiales nostri teneantur jurare quod mandata sibi facta per literas nostras pro ecclesiis et personis ecclesiasticis absque difficultate fideliter exequentur."

quod est suum servetur, et vobis, domine rex, corda retineantur istis presertim temporibus [8] subditorum.

In palatio insuper vestro Parisius constituantur aliqui presidentes viri auctoritate, legalitate, maturitate, sciencia et discretione pollentes, qui continue ac qualibet anni parte audiant et sine more dispendio expediant querelantes tam de negociis et causis regiis quam aliis quibuscumque, absque acceptione aliqua personarum.[9] Et littere que ab ipsis presidentibus concesse fuerint et signate, a vestro cancellario sine difficultate qualibet sigillentur, sic quod subditi curiam vestram diu sequendo non aflicianțur inanibus laboribus et expensis, et quod vestri officiales litteras a vestra curia impetratas absque dampno more executione demandent. Insuper quod predicti in palacio presedentes aliis negociis minime impleantur.

Super articulo vero subsidii seu adiutorii pecuniarii prelati sic respondent predicti quod pro facto monete ac subsidio guerre vestre parati sunt vicesimam partem reddituum suorum unius anni celsitudini vestre dare modis et conditionibus quibus vobis fuit concessa per vestros prelatos et barones qui tunc erant presentes et a vobis liberaliter acceptata verbotenus in Quadragesima proxima precedenti.[10] Et quia inter cetera ibidem actum fuit de mutatione monete, quia ex mutatione huius, si subito fieret, multum dampnificarentur homines regni vestri maiores, mediocres, et minores, suppli-

[8] Probably a reference to the battle of Courtrai and the quarrel with the pope.

[9] This may refer to the *maîtres des requêtes.* They had existed since the time of St. Louis but A. Guillois, *Recherches sur les maîtres des requêtes de l'hôtel* (Paris, 1909), pp. 31 ff. finds evidence of an increase in their activity and a definition of their functions about 1305. He says that the difference between *maîtres des requêtes de l'hôtel* and *maîtres des requêtes du palais* was not clearly established until 1316, but our document seems to refer distinctly to the latter group.

[10] *Ord.*, I, 369. The conditions stated in the ordinance are that no other service or payment shall be taken this year, that supplies seized for use of the army must be paid for in cash, and that no tax shall be taken for reforming the currency. Most of these are repeated below.

cant supradicti prelati per vos aliquod tempus conveniens assignari, usque ad quod moneta que nunc currit habeat cursum suum.[11]

Aliam insuper vicesimam vobis obtulerunt et offerunt prelibati prelati, sed ne periculum apostolice constitutionis incurrant sub conditione,[12] si eis aliquas gratias regalis munificentia duxerit concedendas: videlicet, de amortizandis absque alia finantione acquisitis usque ad nunc per ecclesias regni vestri.[13] Item, quod homines regni vestri dare possint ecclesiis vel legare, sine finantione aliqua vobis danda, pro instituendis capellanis vel anniversariis faciendis de bonis suis aliqua moderata, absque deformatione feudorum et diminutione serviciorum celsitudini regie debitorum.[14]

Fuit autem actum inter cetera quod prelati prefatum subsidium exhibentes ire vel mittere ad exercitum isto anno pro quo dictum subsidium exhibetur vel aliud pro eo prestare subsidium minime tenerentur. Vere cum temporibus vestris in hominibus ecclesiarum quedam novitas sit inducta, videlicet quod ad exercitus vestros Flandrie ac Wasconie ire vel mittere vel se redimere per vestros curiales dicti homines sunt compulsi, faciendo nomine vestro banna et preconizationes in terris prelatorum ipsorum sine voluntate, immo et contra voluntatem eorum, quod nunquam alias anteactis temporibus factum fuit, supplicant supradicti prelati eis concedi litteras

[11] *Ord.*, I, 441, when the currency was finally reformed in 1306 three months warning was given.

[12] The pope had forbidden the French clergy to give any more money to the king in 1301. The purchase of valuable privileges was not a gift, and hence the prelates were not directly disobeying their superior.

[13] *Ord.*, I, 407 (ordinance for the Church of 1304), paragraph 2. "Quod omnia conquesta a tempore retroacto usque ad tempus concessionis presentis in feodis . . . nostris aut subditorum nostrorum tenere possint perpetuo absque coactione vendendi, vel extra manum ponendi, aut financias prestandi nobis pro eisdem."

[14] The right to acquire land freely for church buildings and cemeteries was substituted during the winter of 1303–4 by church councils for the request given here, and was granted in paragraph 3 of the ordinance for the Church of 1304.

regias quod pro premissa vestro tempore innovata ecclesiis vel earum hominibus preiudicium nullum fiat et quod a similibus cessabitur in futurum.[15]

Videtur autem multum expediens quod predictorum adhesio et approbatio a subditis vestris tam clericis quam laicis haberetur priusquam eis fieret mentio de subsidio pecuniario faciendo. Hoc autem offerunt predicti prelati sub modis et conditionibus alias positis et scriptis per manum magistri Amici.[16] Quarum conditionum maior pars superius continetur, illa excepta in qua fuit actum quod moneta parisiensium et turonensium parvorum reduceretur ad statum in quo erat tempore sancti Ludovici, avi vestri; et quod dicta moneta non mutaretur sine magna et inevitabili necessitate, de qua necessitate per vos per fidem vestram et per juramentum consiliariorum vestrorum de secreto consilio qui necessitatem illam scire deberent, vel maioris partis ipsorum, fidem facere deberetis; quo facto, de consilio et consensu maiorum baronum et prelatorum mutationem monete facere possetis, necessitate durante; necessitate vero cessante monetam reducere haberetis ad statum debitum absque gravamine et exactione qualibet subditorum.[17] Item, fuit actum quod predictam conventionem monete vos, domine rex, saltim per alium, et quilibet sucessorum vestrorum regum Francie per

[15] *Ord.*, I, 408, paragraph 11, "quod non est intentionis nostre, nec volumus, quod pretextu exactionum quarumlibet in terris dictorum prelatorum ex parte nostra pro necessitate guerrarum factarum a personis subditis vel justiciabilibus sibi de consuetudine vel de jure eis vel ecclesiis aut personis aliquod generetur prejudicium, vel novum jus nobis propter hoc acquiratur"; paragraph 14, "quod nihil occasione subventionis noviter nobis concesse levabitur ab hominibus ecclesiarum de corpore, seu de manu mortua, alto et basso ad voluntatem talliabilibus."

[16] L. Perrichet, *La grande chancellerie de France* (Paris, 1912), p. 545, Master Amy d'Orleans was a chancery clerk, royal notary 1301–1318, *clerc du secret* 1316, *maître des requêtes* 1318.

[17] *Ord.*, I, 407, paragraph 1, "Quod nos monetas nostras ad statum in quo erant tempore beati Ludovici avi nostri infra annum . . . reduci faciemus, non mutandas amplius nisi urgente necessitate cum consilio prelatorum et baronum nostrorum, qua cessante, iterum ad statum debitum reducentur."

seipsum in coronatione sua deberetis iurare inviolabiliter observare, et quod de hac conventione quilibet episcopus et quilibet magnus baro patentem litteram regiam posset habere si vellet.

Endorsed Declaratio prelatorum super facto monete [*and in a new hand*] que non fuit

APPENDIX III

THE DOCUMENT printed below is in the Archives Nationales, JJ 36, fol. 48 v°, no 123.[1] Officially it is a summons, sent to the leading nobles of Champagne, ordering them to appear in arms at Arras on Tuesday after Pentecost. Apparently the government felt that the response to this summons might be bad, since large sums were still owed to the nobles for services in previous campaigns. Therefore it tried to assure the nobles that enough money would be collected to pay them promptly. They are reminded that representatives of their group are soon to meet to discuss an aid for the war, and are promised that this aid will be sufficient to pay their expenses. There is a suggestion, but no positive pledge, that money collected in Champagne will be used primarily to pay the nobles of Champagne.

An identical letter (except that the time of the meeting is three days earlier and the place is St. Germain-en-Laye) was sent to the leading nobles of Normandy, and is recorded in JJ 36, fol. 47 v°, no. 120. The actual summons to Lagny and St. Germain are printed in *H.F.*, XXIII, 795-96.

A tel salut.

Comme par le consueil de nos freres et de pluseurs autres granz barons aions ordené à estre à Arraz pour le fait de notre semonse en notre propre persone le mardi apres Penthecoste au quel jour et lieu nous vous prions et requerons si acertes comme nous poons que vous veilliez estre pour l'amour de nous en armes et en chevaus si efforciement comme vous pourrez en tele maniere que nous vous en sachiens gre et que nous en soions mes touz jours plus tenuz a vous que à l'ayde de Dieu nous puissiens à ceste foiz [avoir[2]] fin bonne et brieve à l'ayde de lui; et comme nous ayons mandé aus iii semaines de Pasques de genz de votre acort [3] de Champagne

[1] Professor C. H. Taylor kindly made a transcript of this document for me.

[2] Supplied from the identical letter to the Normans, JJ 36, no. 120.

[3] Dr. Frederick Agard of Princeton tells me that this is probably a mistake for "acors," defined in Godefroy as "affluence, concours, foule." The

à Laigny qui aient pooir pour tous [4] le pais, ausqueles nous beons à parler de l'ayde de notre guerre et de notre fait si comme nous avons fait es autres lieus au quel jour nous entendons meismes à ordener pour vous et pour touz les autres de votre acort à faire tel ayde qui vous devra souffire à vous et à tous les autres pour venir en notre veage, si vous prions et requeront[5] si acertes comme nous poons en la foi et en l'amour que vous avez à nous et au roiaume que vous vous efforciez à ceste foiz si de nous servir que si comme nous avons dessus dit nous en soions mes touz jours plus tenuz à vous et au voz nous et les noz. Donnez à Lorriz le premier jour d'avril.[6]

---

word occurs again in JJ 36, no. 121, "nous aions parlé à vous et à aucuns autres de l'acort de Normandie," where none of the usual meanings of "acort" seem to fit. In these documents the word seems to mean the assembly of feudal lords of Champagne (or Normandy); an assembly very much like the old *curia comitis* or *curia ducis*. The scribe may have wished to avoid these expressions, as incompatible with the royal dignity, and therefore have chosen a rare word.

[4] "tout" in JJ 36, no. 120.

[5] "requerons" in JJ 36, no. 120.

[6] The year is not given either here or in the letter to the Normans. However the documents are associated with others dated 1304 in the register and obviously refer to the campaign of 1304.

ASSEMBLIES OF TOWNS AND WAR SUBSIDY, 1318–1319

BY

CHARLES H. TAYLOR
ASSOCIATE PROFESSOR OF HISTORY
IN HARVARD UNIVERSITY

ASSEMBLIES OF TOWNS AND WAR SUBSIDY, 1318–1319[1]

ONE OF THE main problems involved in the development of medieval representative institutions is that of the use to which early assemblies were put, and of the services which they rendered the monarchy. On that use and those services depended, to a considerable extent, the opportunity for assemblies to develop powers of constitutional importance. It has long been recognized that there was some connection between the growing use of representative bodies and the beginnings of taxation; there is a tendency today to emphasize that connection, and to suggest or imply that the *raison d'être* of early representative assemblies lay mainly in this field of service.[2]

Early French representative assemblies have not yet

[1] I am indebted to the Committee on Research in the Social Sciences, at Harvard, for grants which aided the research in archives necessary for this study.

[2] This point of view is brought out clearly in the article of Carl Stephenson, *Haskins Anniversary Essays* (Cambridge, 1929), pp. 291–312. It has many adherents among English scholars, and has been emphasized recently by the study of G. Haskins, *The Statute of York and the Interest of the House of Commons* (Cambridge, 1935) and by J. G. Edwards, "Plena Potestas," *Salter Essays* (Oxford, 1934), pp. 141–155.

On the larger general question of the origin of medieval parliaments, a much broader approach than any discussed here has been suggested by Professor E. Lousse and is being explored under the direction of an international committee; cf. *L'organisation corporative du Moyen Age* (Louvain, 1937) and earlier studies cited there. That approach, as I understand it, does not necessarily deny the importance of the problems to be considered here.

been closely studied in terms of their functional aspects,[3] and there is need for such a study. It cannot be made, however, until important details of their history are better established. The study undertaken here is designed to contribute toward this by an examination of two large assemblies of French towns, which met in the winter of 1318–1319. There are two reasons which justify fresh attention to these assemblies: first, they were among the first of central or large-scale assemblies of towns to be used in connection with a royal effort to obtain subsidy;[4] secondly, there is enough available

[3] Though Langlois was certainly aware of the problem and has it in mind in his admirable survey of early assemblies: Lavisse, *Histoire de France*, III, 2, pp. 248–282. Hervieu and Picot had another focus of approach in their studies; some of the material which they give can be used for analysis in terms of our problem.

[4] It is necessary at the start to explain that 'central' will be used in this study to connote not merely assemblies that included delegations from all of France, but assemblies that were 'central' in the sense of drawing from a large regional area. This sense is intended to contrast with obviously local assemblies — those for a single *bailliage*, or even such a group of *bailliages* as those of Normandy, which had a tradition of unity. From the standpoint of governmental technique in using representative bodies, it will be assumed that this is a line of fundamental contrast. Our concern will be with the question of how, with what purpose and what results, the French government in this early period used representative assemblies which show larger concentrations than those which had long existed, and been used, in the cadres of local administrative districts.

It should be made clear that this investigation is limited deliberately to such assemblies in connection with *town* representation. This means that some of the questions involved may need to be considered elsewhere in the larger context of use made of assemblies of prelates and barons. In particular, the relation of all types of assemblies to the royal council is an ultimate problem of importance and cannot be discussed here. The limitation thus imposed on the present study may be justified, however, by consideration of the fact that assemblies of the different orders, in this experimental and formative period, had no definite or necessary connection one with the

material to give us some knowledge of what went on in these meetings — some indication of procedure and action.[5] Or, to put it in another way, this is almost[6] the first chance, in the line of French central councils, to see something of what happened in large assemblies of towns called for negotiation of subsidy.

The background for these assemblies is the effort of Philip V to deal with the Flemish problem. The terms of a peace settlement made in 1316 had not been accepted by Flanders, despite the efforts of Philip V to secure their ratification. Conditions on the northern border were just short of a state of open warfare by the spring of 1318, and while Philip V was still trying every method of negotiation, he was by that time preparing for the possibility of war. In a central assembly (or series of central meetings with the different orders) in March–April he had raised the subject of war in council with the magnates and asked them for a subsidy;

---

other; they could be and were handled separately or brought together, and can be regarded as presenting different problems for governmental handling, and separable fields for historical investigation.

[5] Most of this material is unpublished. Most of it was known to Hervieu, *Recherches sur les premiers Etats-généraux* (Paris, 1879), pp. 140–154, especially p. 147, notes, and to Lehugeur, *Histoire de Philippe le Long* (Paris, 1897), p. 367 and p. 408. But their references to it are very summary, inadequate and even conflicting (cf. also the two lines given this set of assemblies by Langlois in Lavisse, III, 2, p. 279, end of first paragraph). Cf. references to parts of this material in H. Prentout, *Les Etats provinciaux de Normandie* (Caen, 1925), I, 87.

[6] I say 'almost' because we do know something, thanks to a single chronicler, of the August assembly in 1314, where subsidy in the general sense of aid for war was discussed. But, as this study will try to show, the connection between the assemblies and financial subsidy is much closer in the case of 1318–19.

they managed to avoid action. At the same period Philip brought the Flemish question before the delegates of towns, explained his views, and dismissed the delegates with the injunction to see that their fellow citizens deliberated on his message and prepared to give aid and council when called upon: i.e., to send instructed delegations to a later assembly which would deal with the question he had raised.[7] During the summer of 1318 Philip assembled military forces, but avoided the final step of opening a war,[8] and still pushed negotiations. At the end of July, he arranged for a number of assemblies, to be held in the fall and winter; these assemblies would seem to represent the continuation of the effort, begun in April, to prepare the country for war.[9] The arrangements made in July and completed by later convocations involved meetings of the nobles of a large part of France, in a series of regional assemblies, and separate regional meetings of the towns of a large section of northern France, and of the towns of the south.[10] Our present concern is with

[7] On all this, cf. Lehugeur, pp. 120 ff., and *Speculum*, XIII (1938), 295–303, where I have attempted to explain the use made of the March assembly as far as the towns were concerned. I have taken the view there that the townsmen were probably not asked for an aid in March–April.

[8] It is hard to interpret his policy here: whether as a result of genuine desire to avoid war until all other possibilities of solving the problem were exhausted, or as a matter of wanting war, but putting it off until he was sure of the support of public opinion, sure of getting the military and financial means of warfare. Cf. Lehugeur, pp. 138–143, on this period.

[9] As noted above, the towns had been warned, when dismissed on April 2, to prepare for later consultation on the Flemish problem.

[10] The southern towns were to meet a week earlier than the nobles of the same region. No arrangement was made (as far as the evidence shows) for consultation with the clergy, and no arrangement for assemblies of nobles and towns of certain sections, notably in central France.

these latter assemblies, made up of representatives of towns from two large areas.[11]

One summons of July 29 was directed to forty-six individual towns in the *bailliages* of Vermandois, Amiens Troyes, Vitry, Chaumont, Meaux, Sens, Senlis, Orléans and Normandy.[12] These letters were transmitted through the bailiffs concerned. In addition the bailiffs were instructed to convoke "the other good towns to whom we have not written" [13] by letters following the style of the royal citation: thus the possible size of the

[11] The assemblies of the nobles have been given relatively more attention by Hervieu (cf. also Langlois in Lavisse) and the outline of their history is fairly clear. For some additional documents and commentary on them, cf. Coville, *Les Etats de Normandie* (Paris, 1894), pp. 42, 341, 343.

[12] *H.F.*, XXIII, 812–813. One town, in the region of Sens, is designated only by the letter M. Counting 'Normandy' as having 5 *bailliages*, this meant that 14 *bailliages* were grouped for this assembly.

The text of the summons (from A.N., JJ 55, fol. 45 (anc. XLVI)) is as follows: "Philippus, etc. . . . a noz amez les eschevins de la ville, salut et dilection. Comme nous aiens a traitier et a ordener sus aucunes besoignes touchanz le bon estat de nostre royaume, la paiz et le grant profit de vous et de touz noz autres subgiez, nous vous requerons, et avec ce vous mandons et commandons, que vous deputez trois ou iiii bonnes personnes, et des plus sages de vostre ville devant dite, les queles aient plain poair de vous de accorder faire et acomplir tout ce qui sera ordene, et les envoiez a nous a la quinzaine de ceste prochaine feste Saint Remy a Paris ou nous entendons lors a estre se dieu plaist, et ce ne lessiez en nulle maniere, et nous rescrivez par le porteur de ces lettres le jour que vous aurez receu ces presentes lettres. Donne a l'abbeye Real delez Pontoise lan de grace mil ccc et xviii, le xxix jour de Juignet . . . [par Barriere]."

[13] I.e., towns other than those "whose names we know": letter of Philip V to the bailiff of Amiens, July 29, in Guesnon, *Inventaire des chartes d'Arras* (1863), p. 57. Arras was given such a citation by the bailiff, September 3. That the summons was enlarged in this way for all regions is very probable: that it was done for southern towns is clear, cf. *infra*. This way of enlarging the summons had been followed in the case of the March assembly of 1318: *Speculum*, XIII (1938), 295. The same method may have been used in other years.

meeting was enlarged very much beyond the list of forty-six towns. The meeting was to take place at Paris on October 15.[14] The letters of convocation are vague as to the purpose of the meeting, though the mention of 'peace' may have given sufficient warning, and many towns had been warned in April to prepare for a later discussion of the Flemish question.[15] The towns were to send three or four men with full powers to accord, do and accomplish whatever will be ordained.

Fifty towns of six southern *sénéchaussées* were likewise convoked by letters of July 29, to an assembly at Toulouse on December 18 (a week before the southern nobles were to meet at the same place). The seneschals were notified by letters of the same date[16] to transmit the summons and to extend them to other "good towns and important places" of their districts to whom the king did not send "special" letters.[17] The form of the letters of convocation is almost exactly the same as in the case of the northern towns. By letters of October 29 the king postponed the meeting of the towns at Toulouse to January 1 (or 8), and the meeting of the

[14] I follow Hervieu here, in taking the feast of St. Remi of *Reims* as the basis for calculation. Lehugeur, p. 367, evidently took St. Remi of *Lyon* (October 28) as the basis, without any apparent justification. On November 11, which Lehugeur assigned as the date of the assembly, the king was presumably at Bourges, involved with the assembly of nobles convoked there for November 1. Cf. the *Itinerarium*; *H.F.*, XXI, 477.

[15] *Speculum*, *loc. cit.*

[16] The form letter, addressed to Mâcon, A.N., JJ 55, fol. 44v is a duplication in Latin of the text given above, note 12, and to give the text here would be merely repetitive. For a list of towns and nobles convoked, cf. *H.F.*, XXIII, 813: also (for Languedoc proper), *H.L.*, X, col. 587.

[17] A.N., JJ 55, fol. 44v. This is the counterpart of the text for Arras (Amiens) mentioned above, note 13.

southern nobles to January 8.[18] In these letters of postponement the king warned the southern towns and barons that he might not be able to attend the meetings in person, and would then be represented by commissioners.

In the period between the issue of summons to these assemblies and the meeting of the first (October 15), the French king had continued to negotiate with the Flemish and had been supported by an ecclesiastical interdict (September).[19] On October 11, a truce, effective until

[18] By a series of letters of this date in A.N., JJ 55, fol. 51 (anc. LII): (a) a form letter for individual nobles (*H.L.*, X, col. 588); (b) a form letter for towns, addressed to the city of Lyon (unpublished: it is found also in B.N., Coll. Doat, LII, fol. 38, Narbonne); (c) a general letter to all seneschals concerned, ordering them to transmit these individual letters to towns and nobles, and to notify other towns and barons, already summoned by the seneschals rather than by individual royal citation, of the change in date; (d) a provision for a special clause to be added in the letters (a, b, c) for nobles, towns and seneschal of Lyon-Mâcon. This clause states that in view of the distance of the trip, the king, wishing to spare them expense and trouble, decrees that they shall not go to Toulouse "*ad presens*." The king will shortly communicate his intentions with their regard. Hervieu conjectured that the nobles and towns of this region were later assembled at Lyon (*op. cit.*, p. 145). Actually, the nobles were summoned to Lyon and Mâcon in April and May following (*H.F.*, XXIII, 823): the towns were visited in January by commissioners under writs used for the central parts of the royal domain (model writ for Saintonge, cf. *infra*, p. 116.)

The individual summons (of October 29) to Narbonne is preserved in the copy made by the officers of the *Burgus*, in connection with their appeal of March 1319, *infra*, p. 192. The register copy indicates Jan. 1 as the date for the assembly of southern towns. There is strong evidence that the copy may be in error here and that the citation was actually for Jan. 8: cf. *infra*, p. 128, n. 48.

[19] Lehugeur, p. 140, implies that Philip V was ready for war and was restrained from "vigorous action" by the pope. There seems to be no direct evidence for this interpretation: it is at least possible that what held Philip back was lack of public support, and lack of means — and that he was waiting for the results of the assemblies called in July.

Easter 1319, was arranged, but as before no agreement was reached on final peace terms.[20]

We know something of what took place in the meeting of northern towns, on October 15, from a series of writs which were issued on January 5, 1319, and were based on the results obtained in the assembly.[21] They are instructions to commissioners (usually the bailiff, or seneschal, and one other man) for each *bailliage* or *sénéchaussée* concerned;[22] these agents were to carry through the business of subsidy which had been started at the assembly.

The writs are addressed to the respective commissioners, and begin by an outline of the reasons which led the king to call the assembly of October 15. According to the preamble, the royal leniency had been shown many times in vain parleys and truces with the Flemish, who always professed desire for reconciliation. It was hoped that peace might be established during the present truce, which would last only to Easter. But the king did not think the Flemish were disposed to peace: therefore, fearful that what happened before would be re-

[20] This truce had been first arranged on July 10, and was supposed to lead to negotiations for a definite peace. The negotiations resulted only in the confirmation of the truce, on October 11. For all this, Lehugeur, pp. 140–144.

[21] Only one of these writs has been published, and while it gives some report of the assembly and is somewhat like the others in form, it happens to be the writ for the regions of central France, which were not represented at the assembly (*Archives historiques du Poitou*, XI, 190–194). It has seemed advisable therefore to give the texts of the other writs, for reference here. *Infra*, Texts, pp. 179–191.

[22] The record in the register (A.N., JJ 55, fols. 54 v–57 v) may not be complete. No provision is made for commissions to Vermandois, or to other *bailliages* of Normany than Caen.

peated, and that when the truce ended the Flemish would persist in their state of disobedience, he wished to take council (*deliberare*) with the inhabitants of a number of cities and towns, on the ways and means by which the Flemish insolence, so costly to the kingdom, could be curbed in case they did not make definite peace. To summarize: how should the French government deal with the Flemish after expiration of the truce? It seems reasonable to take all this as a report of the way in which the business of the meeting was actually introduced to the assembly.

The proctors and syndics of the towns (so the writs continue) met for this business before the king and his council, and there were several deliberations (discussions — *tractatus*) on the subject. At this point the several writs begin to differ, according to the different lines of action taken by regional groups and individual delegations, and we must deal with them separately.

The representatives of Meaux and Provins (according to the writ for the commission to the *bailliage* of Meaux), the representatives "of *some* cities and towns" of Normandy [23] (writ for the *bailliage* of Caen), and the

[23] Why does the Caen writ refer so vaguely here to the towns which had taken action, in contrast to the specific references in some of the other writs? Note the later phrasing in this writ: the commissioners will urge the towns of the *bailliage* to act "according to the example of the other cities and towns of the duchy." It is possible that attendance at the meeting was poor (cf. the fact that only Meaux and Provins are mentioned in reference to their areas, though Bar-sur-Seine had been summoned individually and other towns, presumably, by the bailiff) and that no towns from the *bailliage* of Caen had been present. It is possible that towns from this *bailliage* had actually been present but had not taken action: we know there were such towns, from the writs. It is possible that there was a strong sense of regional solidarity among the towns of Normandy, that the towns of Normandy acted

representatives of Compiègne[24] (*bailliage* of Senlis), offered the king the subsidy of "a certain number of sergeants" either for guarding the frontier or for a decisive campaign to end the war, as might be necessary.[25] As later sections of the writ show, "*certus numerus*

---

as a unit at the assembly (*infra*, n. 25), and that the king would therefore refer to this regional action as the best basis of appeal for local acceptance of the assembly's commitment. But it is possible, finally, that these differences in reference to towns at the assembly are merely matters of scribal variation and must not be given too much significance. In the references to the larger number of *bailliages* (Chaumont and five others that took like action) the formula is simply "several towns" or "cities and towns" of the *bailliages* concerned. On the whole, it would seem to be unsafe to deduce anything definite from these variations. The specific reference to Meaux and Provins is made doubtful as an index of attendance of the other towns of their *bailliage* by later usage in the writ: cf. *infra*, p. 180, n. 4.

[24] It might seem from the style of this writ that only Compiègne and Senlis took action at the assembly, though two other towns (Pontoise and Beauvais) had received individual summons. *Infra*, Texts, p. 183. But again we must allow the possibility that the king picked out the two leading towns for convenience of reference.

[25] Another question which is raised but not answered by these texts is this: did the representatives in the assembly act and negotiate with the king in regional groups (by *bailliages*, or for all of Normandy in the case of that region)? The writs suggest such mode of action at first glance, particularly in the case of Normandy. We can suspect that there was a natural tendency for towns of a region to act together; there are indications of this disposition in two mandates for 1303 (Picot, *Documents relatifs aux Etats-généraux* [Paris, 1901], p. 151: powers to act "*prout alie communitates Albigenses*": p. 173, "*juxta ordinationem aliarum universitatum hujus terre*") and one in 1308 (Lavaur: Picot, p. 698, omits the pertinent section of empowerment which runs "*juxta modum et formam aliorum procuratorum universitatum senescallie Tholose*").

Nevertheless, we know that Compiègne and Senlis acted differently and that in several writs the king allows for the cases of towns which did not take the action indicated for a *bailliage*. Finally, the form of the writs can be misleading: they would refer to the action in terms of *bailliages*, because the writs themselves are to be executed in those regional terms. They could have the same form if the action had been taken in a general meeting where

servientum" probably meant a number of sergeants unspecified at the time and to be determined later.[26] It seems most likely that these offers, of a number of sergeants, meant the offer of money to pay for a certain number, rather than the promise of military groups to be organized by the town and sent to the royal army. In other words, these towns promised to contribute money, which would be assessed in terms of the amount necessary to pay for "a certain number of sergeants." [27]

---

the towns lined up in two or three large groups, according to line of action, or were approached individually.

[26] That is, the towns here concerned did not agree to a regional rate of levy by which quotas would be determined (such as so many sergeants per hundred *feux*, as in Philip IV's levies). There is much evidence for this. (1) The commissioners are to summon the towns, in view of the offer of a "*certus numerus*," to make that number such as to satisfy the king in view of their resources — which implies that the matter was open for settlement by negotiation. (2) In the writs for Meaux and Caen the phrase "*aliquis numerus*" is once used in place of "*certus numerus*." (3) In the writ for Senlis, the town of Compiègne seems to have offered "a certain number of sergeants or anything else pleasing to the king" — phrasing which heightens the suggestion of indefiniteness in the offer. (4) Above all, if the towns here concerned had agreed to a rate of assessment which would determine the quota, it is difficult to explain why the king would not refer to such a rate in the writs to his commissioners.

It would not seem likely from the wording of the northern writs that Meaux and Compiègne (and the towns of that group) had promised a "*certus numerus*" in the form of individual quotas, separate for each town, such as Narbonne's offer of seventy-five sergeants in the south. Against this, in the writs, is the fact that the commissioners are ordered to go to Compiègne and Meaux, as well as to other towns, to determine by consultation what the amount offered will be. There would be no need for consultation of Meaux and Compiègne, if they had made lump-sum offers, already accepted. There are strong *a priori* considerations that argue the same way and will be discussed later.

[27] I should urge the following points in support of this interpretation. (1) The writs for these *bailliages* are actually concerned largely with the matter of raising money to pay for the sergeants. The towns are to collect

the money, with the backing of the commissioners, and it is to be held by a local committee "from whom can be recovered, at the proper time, what has been paid and handed over to them, of this subsidy, for these sergeants." There is not the slightest provision, in the writs, for seeing to it that the towns hired, and prepared to send off, their own contingents. (2) The money collected by the towns themselves is to be turned over to a sort of central committee of local notables for the *region*: this would be a curious arrangement if the towns were to then get back their quotas and hire their own sergeants. (3) The practice of levying money in terms of sergeant-units was familiar since at least 1303–04. In the well-known arrangement of that year with the towns of Rouen (*bailliage*) the towns were to raise the money for sergeants and to pay the money to the sergeants, but the soldiers were to be found by the government: *Notices et extraits des manuscrits*, XX (1865), 2, p. 215. (4) The tables of Mignon show that a financial levy was actually made by government officers in these northern *bailliages* in 1318–19 (*H.F.*, *Documents financiers*, I, 204 ff.). Of course, the accounts of this levy might refer to subsidy of nobles and clergy, so the evidence is not decisive. But Paris (p. 204, no. 1643) is recorded as having made a subvention. Rouen paid in money, according to a reference in B.N., n. acq. fr. 21857, fol. 83 v, an account for the *bailliage*. There are two references in the accounts of Provins for 1320 to *sums of money* paid to the bailiff on account of the subsidy made to the king "*pour cause des frontières de l'ost de Flanders*": Prou and D'Auriac, *Actes et comptes de la commune de Provins* (Provins, 1933), pp. 260–261. The accounts for 1319 itself are not given: the references are to items carried over. Senlis and Compiègne rendered financial subsidy: Viard, *Journaux du trésor* (Paris, 1917), p. 225, no. 1227. St. Quentin paid money to the bailiff in 1319 for the Flemish war: Bouchot and Lemaire, *Le Livre Rouge de St-Quentin* (1881), p. 68, no. XXXVIII.

All this detailed argument is necessary because there is much evidence that towns in this period did occasionally raise and send a contingent of their own to royal armies — *certum numerum servientum* in another sense! St. Quentin furnishes examples: cf. Giry, *Archives anciennes de la ville de St-Quentin* (St. Quentin, 1888), I, 196 (3d item) and 171, no. 193, possibly also p. 150, no. 166. There are many possible examples from the south. In 1323, the seneschal ordered Périgueux to send a "*certum numerum servientum*" to the army, and this contingent is indicated later as one hundred men armed and equipped by the town. There is no evidence that the town had offered these men, and the basis of the demand is not clear: *Mémoire sur la constitution politique de la ville de Périgueux* (1775), *pièces justificatives*, p. 198. How much use was made of such quotas is a controversial question, and involves the possible continuation of something like the old *prisée des sergeants*: some towns may still have owed definite contingents of soldiers

The commissioners were to proceed to the towns in their respective districts, assemble the inhabitants [28] and negotiate the actual amount of the subsidy which had been promised in indefinite terms at Paris. The commissioners were to see to it that the money was collected by the towns, and were given some general instructions on principles of assessment. Among these, the most interesting from the standpoint of this study is the principle that those towns of the *bailliages* which had not been summoned to Paris, or if summoned had not taken action there, were assumed to be liable for the subsidy of

---

subject to royal call, and the crown may have used its right on occasion. However, nothing in the context of our documents of 1318–19 suggests that such a definite right was the basis for the effort of the commissioners to get sergeants. Reference to the Périgueux text will bring out the complete contrast in method and approach. On the military contingents of towns, cf. Stephenson in *Moyen Age*, 2nd series, XXIV (1922), 308 ff., 318 ff. and the older literature cited there; also Ch. Petit-Dutaillis, *La monarchie féodale en France et en Angleterre* (Paris, 1933), p. 215, and bibliography.

[28] Whether this meant an assembly of towns for the *bailliage*, or a procedure of negotiations with individual towns, is not clear from the text, and this was perhaps intentional. In the instructions for local negotiators in 1303, they were given discretion on this matter (*Ord.*, I, 370, notes, first item). Both types of operation were possible as far as earlier practice is concerned.

In the writ for Caen, in speaking of individual assessments, the king orders reference to the rate of payment of the *patria* — which would imply an assembly — but he allows also for alternative reference to other base rates which imply differences from town to town (cf. reference to the rate set by the captains of the towns *or* the greater number of them). As far as the literal meaning goes, the writ suggests individual negotiations rather than local assemblies. But in view of the evidence of procedure in 1303, 1304 and others years (the subject needs more attention than it has received), I think commissioners were likely to operate through assemblies if possible. Action at such an 'assembly' could still have been a matter of individual negotiation with separate towns rather than of dealing with a corporate group for regional terms of payment.

a "certain number of sergeants." [29] The government was working here [30] with a principle [31] by which, in a period when assemblies could never include delegations from all the "*universitates et communitates*" [32] and might

[29] The royal commissioners will demand of these towns "*ut ipsi consimile subsidium nobis prestent quod alie ville maiores seu eorum capitanei nobis prestare ut pretangitur obtulerunt.*" There is a difficulty here in deciding whether "*prestare . . . obtulerunt*" refers to the offer made at the Paris assembly or to the definite settlement fulfilling this offer, which the king assumes in advance will be made by the "*villae maiores*" in negotiation with the commissioners. This difficulty arises from mention of the "*capitanei villarum*" who were not at the assembly, so far as known, and whose role in the negotiations we would assume to be local. There are other problems in connection with these "*capitanei,*" when it comes to the details of local assessment. I do not regard the solution of the above difficulties, however, as essential to an understanding of the main features of this assembly and its results. Whatever the role of the captains of the towns, the government is clearly trying to get the smaller towns to accept the principle that what the "*villae maiores*" do, the other towns are expected to do.

For discussion of the difficulties of detail, here referred to, cf. *infra*, Texts, notes 10 and 11.

[30] This principle could not be used in the writ for Senlis, for there one leading town (Compiègne) had offered subsidy in this form, but the other (Senlis) had promised personal military service. Therefore, the writ leaves it open for towns to follow one or the other example. Nor do the writs for Caen and Meaux treat this principle in quite the same way. In the case of Caen, the writ after implying the principle, recognizes that some towns may not accept it ("*fuerint alique communitates . . . que in subsidio huiusmodi . . . sequi viam noluerint aliarum*") and may prefer to offer personal military service: provision is made for this mode of service. It is not easy to explain why the writ for Meaux apparently took for granted that the principle would be followed, while the writ for Caen did not. It may rest on the possibility that no towns of Caen were involved at Paris in the action credited to "some towns of Normandy": hence the government would be more doubtful of applying the principle. Cf. *supra*, n. 23. But it may have been that the writ for Meaux assumed what the writ for Caen added and specified.

[31] We might call it, from the phrase used in the text, the principle of *sequi viam*.

[32] Particularly when the assembly is central for a large area such as this, involving great expenses of travel.

include delegations from only a few leading towns,[33] the action of the assembly could nevertheless be used to bind towns in general. It is the sort of method which, if successful, would help to transform assemblies of delegates who were primarily agents for individual local municipal corporations into assemblies of townsmen who represented an 'Estate' of the realm.[34]

Apparently, a quite different result was yielded by the assembly in the case of a number of the *bailliages* concerned (Chaumont, Troyes, Orléans, Sens, Amiens, Vitry), in the case of Senlis (city), and possibly in the case of some towns in the *bailliages* of Meaux and Caen.[35] The writ for the commissioners of Chaumont sets the style for this group. The king records, with the same

[33] Cf. the cases of 1312 and 1314 when the delegations may have been deliberately limited to those of the *civitates*: *Études d'histoire dédiées à la mémoire de Henri Pirenne* (Brussels, 1937), pp. 337 ff. There is at least a possibility that the attendance in the Paris meeting of October 1318 may have been small: *supra*, n. 23.

[34] What is encountered here may have been one of the major problems that had to be overcome by the central government before it could get much service from large assemblies. We should like to know how far the principle assumed so readily in the writ for Meaux (but not in that of Caen!) really worked in practice: how far the "*villae minores*" of a region would recognize their liability for commitments made by "*villae maiores*," how far the idea of 'Estates' had been developed. Our evidence permits no answers here: we can only see how the government was operating to meet a particular situation. The same difficulty, of course, existed in the case of the other estates: cf. the action of the nobles of Normandy in February 1319, for another aspect of the problem of 'Estates': Coville, *Etats de Normandie*, pp. 341–343.

[35] The writs for Meaux and Caen when referring to those towns which did not promise a subsidy in terms of sergeants (i.e., money) distinguish between three possibilities: (a) towns not summoned; (b) towns at Paris which offered *no* subsidy; (c) towns at Paris which offered another subsidy, which I take to mean military service. What other possibility is there? But the reference is so casual that it may be a matter of form rather than an indication of any considerable group of towns in this third category.

phrases of gratitude used when referring to the offers of subsidy in the form of sergeants, that the delegates of several towns of Chaumont offered to come with the king and to assist him personally by armed service in the prosecution of a final campaign in Flanders. On the basis of this offer,[36] the commissioners are instructed to go to the towns of the district and to publish notices of preparation for personal military service from all inhabitants, to be tested by musters of all concerned, properly equipped according to means, before the commissioners. The inhabitants are, further, to be warned to hold themselves in readiness for summons to the royal army.[37] The ostensible purpose of this is that the king may know in advance what this general personal service will be worth in amount and quality, in advance of the campaign. Actually, a further series of writs shows that these commissioners were engaged in the general effort to negotiate financial subsidy: the proclamations they were to make, and the musters of all men for service were designed to lead the communities (and individuals) to what had been called in similar efforts "*faire finance.*" The nature of their operations would be similar to the work done after declaration of the *arrière-ban* in such years as 1314.[38]

[36] It should be noted that they do not make this offer for frontier guard-service (in case there was no decisive campaign), as had the towns which offered money for sergeants. The offer is limited to the case of a real military effort to end the war.

[37] There is no slightest provision made in these writs for towns which "were not summoned" or did not offer this aid at the assembly: no indication that the government knows it will have to proceed by the principle of *sequi viam*. The implications of this will be discussed later.

[38] Cf. *Ord.*, XI, 429. For similar operations in 1303, cf. *Ord.*, I, 370 (notes).

This evidence is in a second series of writs,[39] sent out at the same date, to the same commissioners operating in this group of *bailliages* (Chaumont, Amiens, Vitry, Troyes, Orléans, Sens). These writs provide that in case any of the inhabitants wish to pay money (*finare*) instead of rendering personal service (which the writ suggests may prove *tediosa et onerosa!*), the commissioners will make financial arrangements with these people for sending a certain number of sergeants, for a year's service if necessary.[40] For assessing and collecting this subsidy, the writ gives instructions that resemble those in the writs for the *bailliage* of Meaux.[41]

It would seem very likely that all this was understood at the assembly and implied in the offer made by the towns of these *bailliages*: they expected their offer to eventuate in local financial negotiations.[42] The differ-

39 *Infra*, Texts, p. 190. The copy of these writs in the register comes last in the series of documents relating to the assembly of 1318.

40 The phrasing, "*de mittendo certum numerum servientum . . . faciatis financias*" is another argument in favor of the view maintained earlier, that the towns did not raise and send their own sergeants.

41 There is fragmentary evidence that in these *bailliages* the king's officers actually raised money in 1319. The incomplete returns for the subvention of this year in Mignon's tables are inconclusive. They indicate that in one of this group of *bailliages* (Orléans) a financial levy was made (*H.F.*, *Documents financiers*, I, 205, no. 1652), but it is not certain from the mention (though inherently probable) that the towns were involved in the subvention. That Senlis, which offered military service, ended by paying subsidy, is proved by an item in the treasury accounts of 1322: Viard, *Journaux du trésor* (Paris, 1917), p. 225, no. 1227.

42 Particularly in view of the royal techniques for translating individual military service of townsmen into money, used since 1300: cf. *supra*, n. 38. There is plenty of evidence, as discussed earlier, that towns occasionally furnished (at royal demand) a contingent of their own troops for the royal army. But that is not what the townsmen of these districts had offered, or (according to either set of writs) were expected to furnish. There is no

ence in ultimate results between their response and that of the first group of towns (Meaux *et al.*) would then be very slight; in both cases, the towns approved the principle of aid and promised aid in a way that would lead to payments of money. But in the case of the Meaux group, this promise, while indefinite as to amount, was good whether or not there was an offensive war, and so gave a basis for immediate negotiations to settle the amount. In the case of the Chaumont group, the promise of personal service was conditional on the undertaking of a decisive (i.e., offensive) campaign; the translation of the personal service into 'finances' could therefore be delayed until it became clear that there was a real war and a real effort — i.e. until the moment when in other years a summons for the *arrière-ban* would have been issued. The form of offer made by the Chaumont group would permit delaying final subsidy commitments to the last possible moment.[43]

Some of the towns at the assembly, finally, would seem to have taken no action whatever on the question

precedent, to my knowledge, for the actual use by the government of military service of individuals in the terms literally suggested by convocation of the *arrière-ban*, or by the first of the writs to this Chaumont group. That occasional individuals preferred to take the demand literally and thereby avoided payment is possible: that townsmen or government ever expected this to happen on any large scale could not be supported by evidence.

[43] Which is just the sort of delayed-action offer we would expect from a population which had reason to suspect the royal 'campaigns to end the war' — on the basis of methods and results in 1313, 1314, 1315 and 1316. One of the general causes for the resistance to the levy of 1314 may have been that most of it was collected (on the basis of a general military convocation) after people knew there had been no real campaign, and that only an unsatisfactory truce had been arranged: *infra*, p. 160.

of subsidy.[44] The commissioners were to approach them on the assumption that, like towns overlooked in the convocation, they would recognize their liability to the subsidy promised at the assembly. We have no means of determining how large this group was.

On the way in which the northern commissioners carried out their financial negotiations (and on results) I have found little evidence [45] beyond the incomplete indications in Mignon's inventory of a subvention for the Flemish war in 1319.[46]

[44] They are referred to in the writs for Caen and Meaux. They are not mentioned in the writs modelled on Chaumont's text, because (as will be argued later) the offer made by these towns was hardly more than what the king was prepared to demand whether offered or not.

[45] There is an expense account for John of Paray, one of the commissioners for Meaux, in B.N., ms. fr. 23256, fol. 42. The account covers ninety-two days of activity, from Jan. 16 to April 17. At first, the expenses are itemized for each day, and permit working out an itinerary, but after two weeks of this only total expenses are given and no itinerary can be made. It is, therefore, impossible to use this account as evidence to determine whether the commissioners negotiated by a local assembly, or by visits to different towns and districts of the *bailliage*. John of Paray claimed 184£ 5s. 4p. of expenses for the whole period of his commission.

[46] In December and January Philip V ordered his seneschals (*H.L.*, X, col. 597) and bailiffs (Hervieu, p. 243) to send him lists of towns in their districts, and also the names of prelates and barons. These orders have been interpreted as evidence of the royal desire to have a more complete basis for the issue of summons to central assemblies; cf. Lavisse, III, 2, pp. 279–280. This was not, I suggest, their main purpose.

On analysis, the text falls immediately into two parts. In the first, the royal officers are ordered to prepare a list of all towns, even those so small that they have no parish church and therefore are hardly to be considered in relation to possible summons to central assemblies. They are to be described in a way that brings out their "estate and condition" — i.e. their relative importance. Those in the royal domain are to be separated carefully from those in seigneurial territory. Haste and, above all, secrecy are prescribed. When we consider these points in connection with the date of the instructions (January 4 for the northern officers, one day before the issue

On the meeting of towns at Toulouse in January there is little more than the evidence from a curious document which records the action of Narbonne's representatives after the assembly.[47] The town (*burgus*) sent delegates with full powers to "agree, do and fulfill," as was ordered in the summons. They appeared before the commissioners of the king,[48] who divulged the royal

---

of writs for our commissioners) everything suggests that the information desired is related to the forthcoming local operations to obtain subsidy.

The second section of the instructions is clearly separate and has the appearance of dealing with a secondary matter, as though the central government used the occasion to get some other information at the same time. "Since we often have occasion to write to" prelates, nobles and notables, towns and places, the royal officers are to furnish the names of these, and the title or office of the town authorities (i.e. whether mayors or *jurés* or *échevins*). This sort of information may very well have been wanted for future reference in case of assemblies, but it could not have been desired for immediate summons. All the assemblies of nobles and towns which the king planned to hold at this period had already been called. The February assembly of northern nobles had been summoned by letters of November 12; the towns of the center were not going to be called at all.

[47] The text is found in B.N., Coll. Doat, LII, fols. 37 ff. It has been summarized, not altogether satisfactorily, in *H.L.*, IX, 381. The text contains a copy of the royal summons to Narbonne (letters of October 29): *infra*, Texts, p. 192.

[48] The text here makes no reference to the presence of any other delegations and if taken literally would convey the impression of an isolated consultation. This may be indicative of the way in which the delegations were actually approached — or it may be simply a false impression resulting from a choice of phrase by a scribe who was not concerned with details of the assembly.

At one time, I thought that this point might be explained by the fact that Narbonne received a summons for January 8, while the form copy in the royal register shows a summons for January 1: in other words, by the possibility that Narbonne, due to a mistake in the date in its individual citation, came a week after the assembly convened, and possibly after its dismissal. But this interpretation is rendered unlikely by an item in the unpublished register of financial accounts of Martel (Departmental Archives

"pleasure and intentions." Narbonne's delegates, with permission of the commissioners, reserved the questions for consultation with their community,[49] and were assigned a certain day (the interval of time is not given) to make answer to the commissioners. On that day they appeared at Toulouse, and the form of their answer shows that the question of subsidy had been raised. They offered, despite the poverty of the town, to send seventy-five armed men for three months, at the town's expense, to help the king if and when he should have a war in Flanders.[50] But the commissioners (the bishop of Laon and the Count of Forez) refused to commit themselves on this offer before the expected arrival of the Lord of Sully, then at Avignon on royal

---

of the Lot, Martel, CC 2, fol. 118r). Martel records expenses of the consuls, who were cited to Toulouse on the *quinzena* of Christmas (January 8) and who stayed there *sixteen days* waiting for the arrival of Sully, royal commissioner. That the two cases we have of the date as actually received by towns could represent a scribal error in transmitting the summons seems very unlikely. Yet that the date as given by the royal register (A.N., JJ 55, fol. 51) as January 1 is a copyist's error is almost impossible, because it occurs in two texts (nos. 104 and 106), and in the latter case by phrasing that brings out an intentional contrast between the date for the towns and the date for the nobles! The only solution I can offer is that the date was changed from January 1 to January 8 after the form letter had been drawn up from which the register got its copy. Note that Narbonne's summons is dated October 29.

49 One of the clearest indications of the fact that delegates with full powers were liable to plead necessity of referring back. And, in this case, Narbonne had presumably been warned in advance of the business of the meeting by the assembly of March 1318. On this and the problems involved, cf. *Speculum*, XIII (1938), 299 ff.

50 The wording here suggests a contingent actually sent by the town, rather than a money payment for a contingent. But the latter interpretation is not barred, and in the absence of other evidence the question cannot be settled.

business. He (they said) was better informed of the royal desire and intent on the business:[51] in other words, the commissioners were not ready to say 'yes' or 'no' to a definite offer of subsidy made some time after the assembly! The delegates of Narbonne repeated the offer to the Lord of Sully when he arrived at Bêziers on his way to Toulouse. He in turn refused to commit himself and ordered another deputation to Toulouse (to the great expense of the town!).[52] This delegation gave the same answer (March 6) before the three commissioners. The offer was finally judged inacceptable, and all the inhabitants of Narbonne able to bear arms were ordered to prepare for personal service and to appear at Arras on April 1![53] The consuls of Narbonne appealed on March 14 from this order on

[51] "*Qui ut dicti domini magistri dicebant, super premissis melius sciebat regium beneplacitum.*"

[52] The date of this final answer gives some clue as to the time of Sully's arrival at Toulouse. It was probably not more than a week or two before March 6, when Narbonne's delegation followed him there to give final answer. This means that he arrived some six weeks or more after the date when the assembly met, and adds to the evidence that the assembly could not have accomplished definite results, since the other commissioners were waiting for Sully: cf. the notice of Martel that its delegation waited sixteen days for the arrival of Sully (*supra*, n. 48).

I have been unable to get further evidence to fix the itinerary of Sully, though there is a great deal of information about him in the registers. A.N., JJ 59, fol. 94v has an expense account for his trip to Avignon and Toulouse, but no dates. He can be placed at Toulouse after March 6 (cf. JJ 56, fol. 138 and fol. 45), but was at Cahors late in March (*infra*, n. 56). Martel gave him a present when he left 'for France': Departmental Archives of the Lot, Martel, CC 2, fol. 118v.

[53] Here we have the familiar technique for applying pressure; the technique which the commissioners in certain northern *bailliages* were to apply to towns which did not follow the example of the offer of sergeants made at the assembly.

various grounds, none of them very impressive — especially the allegation that the commissioners were commanding something at variance with the announced purpose of the assembly, as given in the writs of convocation![54] There is no indication of the outcome of the appeal.[55]

Aside from this text, the evidence from the south throws light only on the way in which subsidy was collected in the spring and summer of 1319, without making it clear what results were obtained from the assembly in January.[56] So slowly were the collections

[54] "*. . . super quibusdam bonum statum regii et utilitatem subditorum et pacem tangentibus. . . .*"

[55] The authors of the *H.L.* (IX, p. 384) cite a text (which I have not found in the archives of Narbonne) which according to the analysis shows pretty clearly that in the end Narbonne (whether city or *bourg*) raised money for war subsidy.

[56] A text from Cahors accords with the suggestion made by the Narbonne document that definite results in the matter of subsidy came much later than January, and presumably after individual and local negotiations: B.N., Coll. Doat, CXIX, fol. 48. Henry of Sully records that the consuls of Cahors promised "*non ex debito sed de gratia speciali*" a subsidy to the king for the Flemish war and that no prejudice shall come to them in the future from this offer. This is the sort of letter which the northern commissioners are instructed to give when negotiations led to a grant, and is dated Cahors, March 28, 1319.

The consular accounts of Martel (*supra*, n. 48) likewise suggest negotiations that only began at the assembly. They record a two-weeks' stay at Toulouse waiting for Sully — and further, they record the expenses of a separate delegation of two men to Toulouse. The date and business of this second delegation are not given, but from the position in the register of several items of expense concerning this delegation, it came after January and was probably concerned with business of subsidy. It stayed eight days at Toulouse, which was not a town with which Martel had ordinary administrative or business relations requiring despatch of such a delegation.

There are several references in Mignon to levy of the subsidy, and they indicate that collection had begun by March and April in the *sénéchaussées*

made, that in some regions only half the amounts promised by towns had been raised on September 13, when peace negotiations were under way.[57]

The king may have planned an assembly for the towns of central France. However, on January 5 when he appointed the commissioners for northern districts, he issued writs of commission for the seneschals of Poitou,[58] Saintonge, Lyon-Mâcon, and for the bailiff of Bourges. These writs follow very closely the form of those of the north. They tell of the assembly at Paris and describe the results in terms of two kinds of offers made: some towns offered a certain number of sergeants and others preferred to offer personal service in an offensive campaign. The king has put off calling

---

of Toulouse, Périgord-Quercy, Carcassonne (*Inventaire de Robert Mignon*, nos. 1684, 1687, 1692, 1693). For Beaucaire, see the following note.

The nobles of Périgord-Quercy made a grant in terms of definite rates but only several months later: *Ord.*, I, 694 ff. (July).

57 *H.L.*, X, col. 604. I have been able to check several documents of Montpellier (thanks to the courtesy of the archivist, M. O. de Dainville): nos. 3862–4 in the *Inventaire des archives communales*, I. They indicate that Montpellier had offered at a time not specified 1500 l. and that some other towns of the district had offered other sums, which allows the inference that the subsidy here took the form of separate grants of lump sums, by individual towns, and was not levied on the basis of general rates. The subsidy was to be paid within the year ending May 1320 and the seneschal is ordered to collect it by urgent letters of August 1, 1319. Again the suggestion is of subsidy as a result of individual arrangements.

I have consulted the texts referred to in *H.L.*, X, col. 602, note; especially the orders of August 13 to the southern seneschals (JJ 58, fol. 44 v, no. 424). They cover subsidy in general, from nobles and towns, and indicate that not all elements had yet offered subsidy, but throw no light on the earlier assemblies. The authors of the *H.L.* (IX, p. 383) assert that the nobility and towns of the south "marched to the aid of the king" as well as contributing finance, but this assertion cannot be controlled.

58 Published in *Archives historiques du Poitou*, XI, 190-194.

before him the people of these central districts, wishing to spare them expense and trouble. He hopes the townsmen of these districts will show no less devotion to the monarchy; the commissioners are to proceed to the towns and treat with their inhabitants on offering a certain number of sergeants.[59] The form of the text shows very clearly that this is what the commissioners

[59] The writs imply that the towns of the center are expected to do as much as had the towns of the north. The king cannot express himself in a way which assumes that the central towns are bound by the consent of the Paris assembly to the principle of subsidy (as he does in the case of towns of Meaux, cf. *supra*, n. 30): he can only hope that they will follow the example set at Paris. The principle involved is that of example, not of virtual representation; for another instance cf. A.N., JJ 58, fol. 45 (1319), where church councils in the south are to be told in detail what offers provincial councils had already made in the north — as a suggestion of example.

The king takes the trouble to excuse himself for not convoking the central towns, alleging his desire to spare them expense and trouble. This does not necessarily imply any constitutional principle which would oblige the king to negotiate consent in an assembly before proceeding to local operations. The king had dealt in person with the northern towns, when he asked them for aid; the northern towns had had the benefit and honor of direct consultation on the policy which they endorsed in principle. Philip V expects his central towns to do as much as the northern, to follow their example, although they had not had the benefit of first-hand explanation of the royal policy; they were being approached by underlings. He wants to counteract any impression that the northern towns have had more favorable treatment.

The same note is struck, I suggest, in his statement in the letters of convocation of the assembly at Toulouse. In the summons of July 29, he hopes to be present: in postponing the summons of October 29, he specifies that the commissioners whom he sends are members of his "greater secret council" — information perhaps designed to impress the southerners with the importance of the commissioners and (I suggest) to atone for the non-appearance of the king.

The same motive, I suggest, is to be inferred from the writ of 1326 in which Charles IV sends commissioners to seek subsidy in Burgundy and justifies himself for not having called the nobles and towns of Burgundy to the central council at Meaux which had endorsed the principle of aid. *Infra*, Appendix.

will put first: then, if some towns do not want to offer sergeants, preferring to aid the king by personal service (i.e., if the commissioners cannot get an offer of sergeants!), they are to be ordered to prepare for this service and to be mustered.[60] The detailed directions of procedure for the commissioners in the two cases are almost exactly like those of the northern writs issued on the same date. We have here provision for local negotiations on subsidy with regions that had not been in any way represented at the Paris assembly; these negotiations were to proceed along very much the same lines planned for regions which *had* been represented at Paris.

Let us now attempt a summary of results obtained from the assemblies we have considered. The Paris assembly committed the towns present (and through them, to some extent, other towns of their *pays*) to the principle of aiding the king in the event of a war with Flanders.[61] But the *amount* of the aid was left entirely unsettled,[62] so that on this important matter the government was forced to local negotiations in order to get definite grants, whether from individual towns or in terms of general rates for a region. In those regions

[60] The implication here is pretty clear. The least the towns can do is to offer the personal military service. As the commission for Caen showed, the king was prepared to demand it whether offered or not.

[61] The maximum obtained here (Meaux, Normandy, Compiègne) was the principle of aid for defensive purposes in guarding the frontier, even if there was no major offensive action by France. Some towns may have refused any commitment at the assembly; their numbers cannot be estimated, *supra*, n. 44.

[62] I.e., in so far as any general rates are concerned. I have considered above the possibility that some individual towns had made individual quota-offers, and concluded that this was unlikely: *supra*, n. 26.

where towns had promised a "certain number of sergeants" the commissioners could proceed at once to negotiate for fixing the quotas (and thereby the amount of money); but in the case where the towns had promised only personal military service in an offensive campaign, the commissioners would be forced to approach finance in a more indirect way, through holding of musters and the threat of enforcing personal military aid.

The picture is much less clear in the south, where there is only fragmentary information on the assembly at Toulouse and its results. But if the towns at the assembly, whether for the whole region or for the district of Narbonne, had made a grant in specific rates, reference to such action would be expected in Narbonne's description of the proceedings. The unwillingness of the commissioners to accept Narbonne's individual offer until the arrival of Sully, the probability that Martel sent a later delegation to negotiate at Toulouse, and the rest of the evidence, suggest that subsidy was ultimately secured by later and more or less local or individual negotiations. The evidence is against the assumption that the Toulouse assembly attained more definite results than did the assembly of Paris.[63]

The significance of these assemblies for constitutional history cannot be estimated merely by reference to their results. It depends largely on how far these results fulfilled the government's expectations or pur-

[63] Cf. the discussion of the evidence, *supra*, p. 132. As stated there, the indications are that towns later made individual commitments of the sort that Narbonne proposed at Toulouse but which the commissioners were not ready to deal with. The question of whether the commissioners at Toulouse tried to get a grant in terms of a general rate for the region is a separate problem and will be discussed later.

pose in using the assemblies. There would seem to be two main possible objectives of government policy. First, the main concern may have been to secure consent to the principle of subsidy, leaving the negotiation of specific rates and amounts for local commissioners. This was substantially the measure of results actually obtained at Paris.[64] This would mean that the central assembly was designed to do some of the work that would otherwise have to be done by local negotiations, but not the main part, for no commitments would have been made on amount. This use would represent a

[64] Whether the assembly promised subsidy in terms of money for sergeants, or in terms of personal service (later to be translated into money) is not essential.

I am aware that this apparently overlooks the difference between what was obtained from the Meaux-Compiègne-Norman group on the one hand, and the Chaumont group on the other. At first glance this difference may seem considerable. The first group promised subsidy whether for offensive war, *or* for garrisons and defensive operations on the Flemish frontier for a year. The second group promised only aid (i.e., personal military service) in case of an offensive campaign to settle the Flemish issue decisively. The king would obviously have preferred the first type of offer, and in that sense could be represented as only partially satisfied with the results of the Paris meeting.

However, this difference in results, though real, seems of very minor import when contrasted with the difference between a grant of a subsidy in terms of a definite rate, and the indefinite promise of a subsidy which left amounts to be settled by further (and as events proved) protracted local negotiations. Furthermore, that the success or failure of the assemblies was measured by attainment or non-attainment of what Meaux, Compiègne and Normandy gave (subsidy for frontier defense as well as offensive war) would argue that the king did not know whether he wanted to undertake an offensive war or not! This seems extremely unlikely in view of his proposal to the spring assemblies of 1318, and in view of the fact that he called the assemblies at all. Philip may not have been sure that he would be able to undertake the war; from this standpoint, the Meaux offer was an anchor to windward.

technique of preparation for local negotiations, something added to them in order to assist them.

Or, the government's objective may have been much more than this. The king may have hoped to get not merely consent to the principle of war subsidy, but agreement on a definite rate of subsidy,[65] either for the whole region represented by the assembly, or separately for its larger units, such as the *bailliages*. This was the type of grant which Parliaments had long since made to English kings. With such a grant secured, the main work would be done; local negotiations would be little more than application of the general rates, and care for the details of assessment and collection. The main burden of securing war subsidy would be shifted from the operations of local commissioners to the handling of the large regional assemblies. As techniques of administration, these two possible objectives offer a clear contrast: the difference in implications for constitutional development is almost equally clear.

Taking these as the two main possible interpretations of the government's policy, we may allow for a minor variation of the first. Assuming that the basic objective was to secure consent on the principle of subsidy in the central assemblies, as an opening to local negotiations, the government might also be willing to entertain definite *offers*[66] by individual towns, at the as-

[65] In some such terms as those which the government tried to *impose* in 1302–04; a rate of so many sergeants (at a money equivalent) *per* hundred hearths, or a rate in terms of proportional payment on income.

[66] I.e., offers of a lump sum, or of a definite quota of sergeants, which would mean the same.

sembly, and in anticipation of the local work; to begin, where occasion offered, the sort of negotiation with particular towns that the commissioners of subsidy were to conduct in northern *bailliages*.

We must at least keep this possibility open because of the record of Narbonne's actions, in the meeting before the royal commissioners at Toulouse. Narbonne's delegates heard the commissioners, asked for delay to consult the town council, and then made a definite offer of seventy-five sergeants. The first apparent implication of this action is that Narbonne made such an offer because the commissioners had asked for it. On further analysis, however, the evidence gives much less than decisive support to such an inference. When Narbonne made its offer, the commissioners refused to accept or to decline it; they alleged that they must wait the arrival of Sully, who was better informed of the royal wishes.[67] This does not suggest that they were ready to press the towns at the assembly for definite commitments in any form, and the first impression made by Narbonne's offer is more or less neutralized.[68]

[67] Note also the evidence from Martel: its delegates were sixteen days at Toulouse, waiting for Sully (and Sully did not get there in that interval!); *supra*, n. 52.

[68] We may offer two other possible explanations of Narbonne's offer, which may have better chances of fitting the evidence:

(1) The commissioners may have been mainly concerned with getting consent on principle: and this may have been what Narbonne was supposed to give answer on. But the commissioners may have suggested the possibility of making final individual offers, without really expecting to get response at the moment. Narbonne's reply would find them unprepared.

(2) Narbonne, asked to merely pledge subsidy, may have seen an opportunity to profit by the occasion and to escape with a small payment by making an immediate definite offer. The commissioners might not be in a

The direct evidence is, therefore, inconclusive. Furthermore, on *a priori* considerations it does not seem likely that the government would have made a main point of concluding final individual settlements at the assembly, nor that getting such settlements would have been a main consideration in the use of the central assemblies. We shall see later that there is very great reason to believe that the government would have, at this time, unusual difficulties in getting final commitments from such assemblies, definite commitments in any form;[69] we shall also see that the government could be expected to know this. But while the difficulties of getting final commitments would be comparable, no matter which *form* the commitments took (individual offers or general rates), the advantages to

---

position to appraise its adequacy. The whole tenor of Narbonne's appeal indicates that Narbonne knew its offer would be considered small.

In any event, the record of Narbonne's offer does not in any way suggest that the assembly at Toulouse had been asked to make a grant in terms of definite *rates*, applicable to the region or even to its main administrative districts. Narbonne's description of its appearance at Toulouse gives no indication of consultation with other towns; one would hardly guess there had been an assembly! Its offer is not in terms of answer to a demand for flat rates. The commissioners' hesitation, and their desire to get the royal policy from Sully, makes it almost inconceivable that they had demanded a definite rate before the assembly. It does not, of course, make it impossible that Sully might have been expected to produce such a policy, when he arrived.

[69] These difficulties will be discussed in full later. They would apply whether the government wanted delegations to give individual commitments (in the form suggested by Narbonne's offer) or commitments in terms of general rates. There would even be an added difficulty in the former case. If the government wanted to press for individual offers, it would mean breaking the assembly into a series of negotiations with the individual towns — a process which would be clumsy and might take an interminable time.

the government would be very unequal in the two cases. If the assembly merely gave a number of individual grants for the particular towns present, then the main work of raising subsidy was still left for local negotiations,[70] for the specific amounts to be given by *other* towns would not be in any way determined at the assembly.[71] If, however, the assembly agreed to a general flat rate of payment in terms of some general principle of assessment, then the main work of securing subsidy was done, and local operations would be a matter of applying and enforcing the principle and rate of payment.

This comparison makes it clear that even if (on account of the evidence from Narbonne, however inconclusive it be) we keep open the possibility that the government was willing to encourage some individual final settlements at the assemblies,[72] this possibility would

[70] Unless we assume that most of the towns of the region were present. But the government made no special effort to ensure this; the seneschals and bailiffs were given only casual general instructions to call other towns than those receiving individual royal letters of summons. Yet the government could, if it wanted to, call directly a much larger list; it had done this in 1316, as will be shown in a separate study of the little-known assemblies of that year.

[71] No more would have been accomplished, beyond establishing the principle of subsidy, than final results *in individual terms* for some leading towns. And it could be argued with some reason that if individual separate settlements were the aim of the government, it would be better to make these locally. Central commissioners were not advantageously placed to judge the adequacy of an individual offer: local negotiators, working with the bailiff or seneschal, were better able to do this.

[72] And whatever Narbonne suggests for the south is further neutralized by the record of Compiègne's offer in the northern meeting. Compiègne apparently promised a "certain number of sergeants or anything else pleasing to the king" (cf. *infra*, p. 183). This does not indicate that Compiègne had been pressed for definite commitment of any sort. The northern writs

not constitute a significant alternative interpretation of governmental policy in using central assemblies. The essential contrast in possible service would be between the central assembly that served as a prelude for mainly local operations, largely by securing consent on principle, and the central assembly that would give grants in definite form that would allow escape from individual and local negotiations over amount.[73]

With the field of possible main interpretations of government policy thus limited, we may begin by consideration of the second of these possibilities. What ground is there for assuming that the French government in 1318–1319, at the assemblies of Paris and Toulouse, planned or hoped to get grants of subsidy in terms of general rates of assessment?

There is nothing to support such an assumption in the direct record of the assemblies themselves. The writs do not indicate that the government had gone before the delegations with a proposal for a definite grant in terms of general rates. They do not show that the government was disappointed in the results actually obtained. Narbonne's offer of seventy-five sergeants, given maximum significance as a possible index of the demands of the commissioners at Toulouse, does not

---

do not suggest that definite individual quotas had been promised by any towns: *supra*, n. 26.

[73] These seem to be the two significant types of possible use. If further evidence came to light and confirmed what is made barely possible by Narbonne's offer, if it appears that the French administration tried to get individual settlements from towns at the assemblies of 1318–19, we would still class this use of the assemblies as a form of the first and more limited type of use. At most, it might be regarded as a slight transitional step from the one type toward the other.

suggest that the commissioners had asked for a grant in terms of a general rate.[74] On the whole, our evidence is compatible with the possibility that such a grant had been sought,[75] but goes no further.

However, some arguments in favor of the larger objective can be found elsewhere: it is possible to draw certain inferences from the wider record of the royal efforts to get subsidy in 1318–1319.

In the first place, there is the fact that the towns of France (or some of them) had been warned in April 1318 to prepare for a royal policy, with regard to Flanders, on which Philip V would seek their aid and counsel: i.e., warned to prepare for discussion of policy that would presumably mean subsidy. These towns (and they may have been numerous) would know what the summons of July 29 meant. Would the king have made preparations of this sort (to secure instructed delegations) if he had expected only the results which were actually attained in the Paris meeting? Do not these preparations argue a royal policy which would aim at getting from large assemblies more than a consent to the principle of aid?[76]

In the second place, there is the fact that in the assembly of November 11 at Bourges, comprising the nobles of Berry, Auvergne, and Nevers, the king secured from the nobles of Berry a definite grant of aid in terms of a rate for general assessment of noble

[74] *Supra*, p. 138, and n. 68.

[75] I.e., in the north, even if the effort had been made, and failed, the government might still (as a matter of tactics) conceal the failure in the writs and express its gratitude for the results actually obtained.

[76] And even that, for several *bailliages*, in a form which postponed commitments as long as possible!

property (a fifteenth). If the king secured that much, it must be because he tried to: if he hoped to get that much from the nobles of Berry, that would make it at least possible that he hoped for as much from the other elements of his kingdom, called to assemblies.

In the third place, there is the record of methods used by the French government in approaching the towns of central France (Bourges, Poitou, Saintonge, Lyon-Mâcon). Instead of calling an assembly for that region (and the king indicates that he might have done so, i.e., it is possible that he planned to do so), Philip V sent commissioners to central France on January 5 with very much the same instructions as those carried by commissioners to the towns of the north. The towns of the center were expected to do as much, or as well, though they had not been assembled before the king, as the towns which came to the meeting at Paris on October 15. Local negotiations were expected to do as well in one region as in the other. Why did the government use a central assembly for northern towns and only local negotiations, by commissioners, for the center? One obvious possible answer is that Philip V had failed to get from the northern assembly results which would make it seem worth while to use the same method in the center: that the king found he could not escape local negotiations with towns, and in the case of central France decided not to attempt it.

These are the main grounds for an interpretation of the results of the Paris assembly which would represent them as less than the government had planned.[77]

[77] Another line of argument in this sense could be based on the differences between the assembly of 1314 and the assemblies (of towns) in 1318–19. This will be duly presented and considered later.

If we turn to the other possible main interpretation, that the results were on the whole satisfactory, that the government was primarily concerned with getting consent on the principle of subsidy, we will again find little in the immediate record of the assemblies of Paris and Toulouse to do more than make such a conclusion possible. However, in the case of Compiègne there is the curious point that this town seems to be reported in the royal writ of commission as having offered a subsidy of a "certain number of sergeants or anything else pleasing to the king." This strongly suggests, at least, that Compiègne could indulge in such vague and generous generalities because no definite commitment was being sought in the Paris assembly.[78] There is, also, the point, small, indecisive, but nevertheless suggestive, that in all the writs of commission of January 5, 1319, the king speaks with terms of gratitude of the offers made by the respective groups of towns — even where the offer is only of personal military service.[79] This may be only a matter of style, or of good tactics glossing over a defeat, but we may wonder why the king bothered to acknowledge with warm phrase an offer of personal military service if his real purpose had been to get definite financial commitments.

It is when we turn from the immediate record of the assemblies to the context, to the general background of the political situation in France, to the earlier record of royal efforts to get subsidy for war, that we come to the

[78] Granted that this is not the only possible inference to be drawn from the expression. Further, it should be recognized that the text is difficult to read at this point — *quodcumque* is not certain. *Infra*, Texts, p. 183.

[79] Though the king indicates elsewhere that he is disposed to take personal military service for granted, as something he can demand: *supra*, n. 60.

strongest grounds for argument that Philip V obtained substantially what he sought from the Paris assembly in 1318: agreement on the principle of aid for war.

The main ground on which the argument will rest here is the contention, which I believe can be very strongly established, that Philip V would have every reason to expect much more than ordinary difficulty in getting subsidy from his subjects, for military purposes, in the winter of 1318–1319.

It is fairly clear to us, and (if true) would have been even clearer to the government, that an appeal for aid in a Flemish war might find a public opinion not merely unresponsive but almost hostile. The country had participated in a long series of military efforts to subdue the rebellious province, had given financial support for those efforts in generous measure, and had seen results which were not liable to arouse either enthusiasm for a new venture or confidence in the government's ability to succeed where failure had been so repeated. The campaign of 1313 had been the start of the second period of wars with Flanders, and had led to nothing. In 1314, the last effort of Philip IV assumed the proportions of a national scandal: not only was there widespread opposition to the payment of subsidy for a campaign which ended in an unpopular truce, there was also general criticism of the government for mismanagement of the war.[80] National pride was perhaps touched, and this would help to account for the otherwise remarkable [81] fact that Louis X was able to raise another army

[80] Artonne, *Le mouvement de 1314* (Paris, 1912), p. 17.

[81] Remarkable in view of the state of public opposition to the war subsidy of 1314 — which was alleged as the general basis of the organized movements which led to the charters of 1315: cf. Artonne, p. 13.

and a new subvention for a campaign in 1315. But this campaign failed as ignominiously as its predecessors, and like its predecessors saw a military effort dissipated without even a battle. That was the end, for the moment, of major campaigns.[82] Philip V as regent in 1316 negotiated, with the result of a new version of the treaty of peace which had first been made in 1305. This later version had the fortune of its predecessors, and was not carried out by the Flemish; but at least there was, after this peace, a period when the perennial campaigns with their demands for money and military service and with their uniform record of humiliating results had come to an end. Would the state of public opinion, given this background, be more likely to resist or to welcome a reopening of military effort: would the king expect to find it more or less difficult than before to get money?

It is hard to get much direct evidence as an index of public opinion to support this line of argument. But what evidence we have in 1318 indicates that public opinion was certainly not enthusiastic for war and may well have been rather opposed to it. In the first place, there is the record of Philip V's effort to get aid for war from an assembly of barons and prelates in April 1318.[83] The prelates put the matter off by refer-

[82] Though Louis X, in the last months of his reign, was trying to prepare a new campaign for 1316. For this purpose, he called assemblies of towns which have been little studied and which I intend to treat in another connection. There is an interesting possibility that he may have planned to use them in the way that (as I shall argue here) the assemblies of 1318–19 were used.

[83] On this meeting, of uncertain date, cf. *Speculum*, XIII (July, 1938), 295 ff.

ring to provincial councils: what the nobles did is not recorded, but since there is no sign of a subvention in that year, the inference is that they declined the request, whether by direct refusal or evasive tactics. Yet, if there had been any strong public opinion in favor of war, it might have been expected to show itself at this moment. The Flemish had just broken off the negotiations for final ratification before the papal court, and border outrages had been taking place during the winter.

Further, there is the record of Philip V's evident unwillingness to bring issues to a head during the summer of 1318. The Count of Flanders had defied the summons to appear (in May) before the Peers, Cassel had been actually taken from a royal garrison, and disturbances on the frontier were almost continuous. Yet Philip continued to negotiate, and apparently hoped for effects from the action taken by the Church; though he assembled troops at Arras (August 5), they were held on the defensive. This might be the policy of a long-suffering friend of peaceful methods,[84] but it could also evidence the caution of a government justifiably uncertain of support from a country which had every reason to be disillusioned about military efforts against Flanders.

Another main consideration, which has some weight in judging whether the government would have high or modest expectations of results from the assemblies of 1318–1319, is the popularity of the monarchy, its probable strength from the standpoint of controlling

[84] Lehugeur's suggestion. On the relations between France and Flanders in this period, cf. Lehugeur, pp. 127 ff.

public opinion. A popular government, or one which was recognized as being strong and determined, would have that much more reason for feeling confident as to the measure of support it could expect for its policies.

There is good reason to doubt that Philip V's government was, or felt itself to be, either strong or popular. Philip V had come to the throne at a period when the wave of popular exasperation with the government of Philip IV had just showed its force — when any government would feel inclined to caution. But to make his situation even less comfortable, Philip had come to the throne by a sort of *coup d'état*: his transformation of the regency into the royal office had been irregular enough to present hazards. As a result, he had made marked efforts to conciliate public opinion and secure public support: by assemblies of various types in 1317, and by measures of conciliation which show his feeling of insecurity. Even then, he had not been able to reconcile a powerful and antagonistic group among the nobles until March 1318.[85] In Artois, there was still a survival of rebellion among the nobles, who had made the league of 1315 a vehicle for opposition to the claims of Mahaud.[86] While there is no index of the towns' attitude toward the government of Philip V, there is no apparent basis for assuming that in this quarter the government could count on enthusiastic support. We have, in short, good reason to infer a general state of public opinion which would be calculated to make the

[85] Lehugeur, pp. 101–102.

[86] Louis of Nevers and Rethel was an ally of Flanders and a source of trouble; any war with Flanders was likely to involve war on his lands in France. For his policy in 1318, cf. Lehugeur, pp. 138–139.

central government feel uncertain, and not overconfident of its ability to carry through difficult policies.

There is still another element in the immediate background to be considered as a basis for estimating the expectations of the government. At the time when the assemblies met (October and January), not only had there been no official reopening of war with Flanders, but a truce had been made (July 10) with the avowed purpose of permitting final settlement of peace. True, such a settlement had not been made (and the negotiations of August and October seemed to indicate that it would not be made), but the truce was to last until April 1319. There was no war, and there would be no war until April. If there is strong ground for believing that the country wanted no war, would a government with merely ordinary ability to estimate realities expect to get definite commitments of subsidy from assemblies held so far in advance?[87]

Philip V and his ministers, in viewing the situation, had more on which to base their estimate of results than awareness of the general state of public opinion.

[87] I have suggested in my study of the April assembly of towns in 1318 (*Speculum, loc. cit.*) that the government knew, by this time, that proctors would avoid definite commitments if possible and that proctors had opportunities for making it possible! Under the circumstances of October 1318 (or January 1319) town proctors had the best of opportunities for declining definite commitment: there was no war and there might be no war. Even the king in his preamble to the writs (representing probably the line of his address to the assembly at Paris) had to argue that he did not *expect* peace to come, rather than that war was inevitable. The whole tone of those preambles suggests an effort to convince people who wanted to avoid war that war might be necessary. This is not the tone of a government that would have expected definite commitments in advance from representatives who were (under any circumstances) liable to be cautious about making them!

They had the experience of past efforts to obtain subsidy, in the case of previous wars, since the period when Philip IV began to experiment on large-scale lines. And this experience would not be calculated to produce optimism as to what could be hoped from such assemblies as were called at Paris and Toulouse. In the first place, once the government (from 1302 on) had practically admitted the need of getting consent to subsidy, at least in the determination of amount and assessment, this consent had been obtained by localized negotiations, often with individual towns [88] and at most, as far as the evidence shows, with the towns of a region as large as a *bailliage* or *sénéchaussée*.[89] Until 1314, there is no evidence that assemblies on a scale larger than this had been used to deal with the towns.[90] In other words,

[88] Cf. the instructions to the commissioners who are sent out in 1303: *Ord.*, I, 370. They are to proceed at choice by negotiations with individual towns, in a town assembly, or with representatives of several towns. For evidence of the latter type of operation, cf. the agreement on subsidy reached with the towns of the *bailliage* of Rouen in 1304: *Notices et extraits des manuscrits*, XX (1865), 2, pp. 156–157.

[89] Where the records of subsidy assessment show a uniform rate for a *bailliage*, I take it to mean that an assembly of towns probably arranged this rate with the commissioners. In the record of 1314 (*H.F.*, XXI, 566 ff.) for instance, this would be the inference for the *bailliage* of Orléans, but not for Touraine (p. 567).

[90] The best possibility that a large concentration had been used is in the case of southern towns in 1304. There was so much opposition to the subsidy announced in 1303 (October: *Ord.*, I, 391) that Philip IV went to Languedoc in December. In some way, he negotiated for consent to such effect that by February he was able to speak of the subsidy recently granted in the (separately named) southern *sénéchaussées*. This might mean a general regional assembly; it might sum up the results of a series of local negotiations that had taken place separately. If the former, it might mean an assembly merely of notables. Dognon, *Histoire des institutions politiques et administratives de Languedoc* (Toulouse, 1896), p. 202 does not hold that

experience up to 1314 gave no assurance for expectation of substantial results from large representative bodies, in subsidy negotiations, because there had been no attempt made to use such a medium of negotiation.

In 1314, for what seems to be the first time, the crown brings the question of subsidy before a central body of town representatives. Here, therefore, is a possible precedent for whatever use was intended for large assemblies in 1318, and this meeting needs careful examination. The sole evidence that we have comes from the Chronicle of St. Denis, but comes in unusually detailed and circumstantial form. On August 1, the king, accompanied by barons and prelates, appeared before a body of delegates from "all the *cités*" of the kingdom.[91] Marigni, as royal spokesman, harangued the

---

the evidence demonstrates a central assembly: in the same sense, cf. *H.L.*, IX, 266. In any event, if there was a large assembly, including towns, before February 1304, it did not make a grant in definite terms, for after that date we have record of local assemblies of towns in the several *sénéchaussées* at which the definite terms were finally made, and only on the basis of royal concessions: cf. *H.L.*, X, col. 432, no. III: Ménard, *Histoire de Nismes* (Paris, 1751), I, 148: *Ord.*, I, 399, 405, 410. If there was a large preliminary assembly, it did not permit the government to escape the necessity of further negotiations on the usual local scale. In the north of France in 1304 the negotiations were apparently local: cf. Funck-Brentano, *Philippe le Bel en Flandre*, pp. 460–461, especially note 1, p. 460.

[91] In other words, apparently the assembly had been formed on the basis of a narrow range of summons, with only the episcopal towns present. The use of the word might be suspected as a matter of carelessness on the part of the scribe, but (1) In 1312 at Lyon-Vienne Philip IV had used the same selective basis of summons for the towns. Cf. *Etudes d'histoires dédiées a la mémoire de Henri Pirenne* (Brussels, 1937), pp. 337 ff. To the evidence there assembled (for southern *cités*) add an expense writ for Arras, which is a counterpart of those for Albi or Périgueux, and shows that the attendance was wide: *Inventaire des archives départementales du Pas de Calais* (1878), pp. 89–90, nos. AA–58, 5 and 59, 4. (2) I do not find elsewhere in the chron-

audience on the past history of the Flemish trouble, on the righteousness of the king's policy and on the expenses and needs of the king. Then, coming to the point (and the king rose to observe the response), he asked "what towns would give him aid and what towns not, to go against the Flemish in military force." [92] The Paris spokesman said in reply (for Paris) that "they were all ready to aid the king each according to his power and according to what would be suitable, to go *where he may wish to lead them* at their own cost and expense against the Flemish." The other towns answered in like vein that "willingly they would aid him." The king thanked them and *that ended the matter*, as far as out text shows. Unless some good reason can be shown for distrusting a remarkably circumstantial account, apparently that of a witness, Philip IV asked for no more than approval of the principle of military aid, without seeking any definite commitment on *either* form or amount, and obtained what he sought.[93] In short,

icle that the word "*cité*" is used in the generic sense of 'town.' (3) If the scribe had meant towns in general, he would hardly have said "*all* the towns (*cités*)" but rather "many" or a "great many" towns.

[92] The text is, ". . . Engerran requist pour le roy aus bourgois des communes qui yleuc estoient assambles quil vouloit savoir lesquels li feroient aide ou non a aler encontre les Flamens a ost en Flandres. . . . Adonc Estienne Barbete bourgois de Paris se leva et parla pour la dicte ville et se presenta pour eulz et dist quil estoient tous prest de faire li aide chascun a son pooir et selonc ce qui seroit avenant et expedient a aler la ou il les voudra mener a leurs propres coux et despens contre les dis Flamens. Et adoncques le roy les en mercia. Et apres ledit Estienne, tous les bourgois qui yleuc extoient venus pour les communes respondirent en autelle maniere que volentiers li feroient aide: et le roy si les en mercia. Et lors apres yceli parlement. . . ." *H.F.*, XX, 692.

[93] If not, if the response of the assembly was an evasive or unsatisfactory one, why did Marigni phrase the question in a way that was so general as

in so far as the assembly of 1314 is concerned, in so far as it would serve to guide policy in 1318, it would give a basis for expectation of just about the measure of results actually obtained in the Paris meeting of October 1318.[94]

As a final possible element of experience which might help to shape the government's expectations in 1318, there is the point that the government had been using local assemblies for negotiations of subsidy since at least 1302, and was presumably aware of the difficulty in getting proctors to make final commitments without reference back to their constituencies.[95] If the govern-

---

to permit an indefinite answer? And why could not the king press the point, once the principle of aid had been approved?

[94] There is need for a warning here on what seems to be misinterpretation of the purpose of the 1314 assembly by Artonne. He says (p. 16) it was to speed up the collection of a levy which was decreed in the winter of 1313 and was not going well. The only evidence for his contention that a levy began then, well in advance of the August assembly, is a reference in Mignon's inventory (*H.F.*, *Doc. fin.*, I, 199) to a decree for a subvention, November 11, 1313. But Artonne overlooked the conclusion of Mignon's note, "Find out if it was collected, because nobody seems to have accounted for it!" This is all we know about the "levy" and the fact that Mignon had no trace of it, and distinguished between it and the very fully recorded levy of 1314 shows that a levy, if planned in November 1313, was not carried out. There is no need for going further and showing the difficulty of reconciling Artonne's hypothesis with other evidence.

[95] For one thing, on the claim of a lack of instructions. The efforts of the government to inform local opinion in advance of a large assembly, in 1318 and 1321, implies that the government knew of the difficulty by this time: cf. *Speculum*, XIII (1938), 299 ff. If so, it must have encountered this obstacle in local negotiations, and there would be nothing surprising in such an assumption. We would not suppose that it was easier to get proctors to make final commitments in the earlier stages of the development of assemblies than it became later. For an almost perfect example of proctorial delay in subsidy negotiations (local) in 1327, cf. Prou and D'Auriac, *Actes et comptes de la ville de Provins*, p. 284.

ment was aware of this problem, given all the other circumstances in the situation in 1318, it would be most surprising if definite grants in any form had been really expected from the meetings at Paris and Toulouse.[96]

To summarize: the state of public opinion was presumably such as to make it harder than usual to get any kind of support for a Flemish war; the government was trying to get money, or at least definite commitments (by local negotiations, if not central), in advance for a war which was not certain to eventuate; and on the basis of experience, the government had no reason (that we can see) for assuming that large assemblies would be disposed to make final grants.[97] These considerations give a solid ground for argument that Philip V in 1318 was not calling large assemblies of

[96] And if the government was not aware of this particular problem it is hard to see why large assemblies had not been used earlier in the attempt to get subsidy, once the government admitted (by its tactics in local negotiations) that it was desirable to get consent. For (1) local assemblies were used for subsidy negotiations, (2) central assemblies had been used for other purposes since 1302, and (3) the example of England, where definite grants had long been made by a central body, must have been known to the French officials. They could hardly have failed to see the obvious practical advantages in swift, concentrated negotiations, *were these judged feasible.*

[97] Even if the government were inclined to experiment, in view of the points just summarized this was not a time when experiment would be advisable.

It is always dangerous to reconstruct motive, and to argue from the probable 'line of reasoning' of an age so different from our own. But in the present argument, while I assume the government would be actuated by rational considerations, the latter are of a lowly and practical order, commensurate with average administrative awareness of what public opinion is, of 'what can be done.' I am not basing the argument on the existence of, and adherence to, any particular constitutional or political theory. What we are concerned with here is a technique, a way of doing something that had to be done.

towns to get from them definite grants of subsidy. Such a purpose might be assumed, *if* the circumstances were such that an unusually favorable response to a request for subsidy could be anticipated; actually, the situation seems to be the reverse.[98]

This estimate of the general background and its conditioning effects will do more than explain the probable limits of Philip's expectations from these large assemblies; it will also explain why, if we assume limited expectations, the king bothered to use these large assemblies at all. This certainly needs explaining, for if we argue that these meetings were not designed to permit an escape from local negotiations they become, apparently, a somewhat futile prelude. However, if local negotiations were expected to be rather more difficult than usual, then such results as the central assemblies gave might have practical importance; they might make the negotiations easier. Our assemblies would then represent a supplementary technique, justified by the presumably difficult situation as an *addition* to the ordinary methods of raising war subsidy.

[98] We might add to this general line of reasoning a good deal of scattered evidence which suggests that the government found it difficult to get subsidy during the local negotiations of 1319. This evidence is not complete enough to justify the claim that unusual difficulties were encountered, but it certainly does not suggest enthusiastic response; i.e., a public opinion more favorably disposed toward war than we have pictured it. For resistance by individual towns, cf. *infra*, p. 161 and note 113. For indications that not all southern districts were responsive, cf. *H.L.*, X, col. 601, and A.N., JJ 55, fol. 70. For the attitude of the nobles in large regions, cf. Hervieu, p. 152 and Coville, *Etats de Normandie*, p. 42. There is a good deal of unexamined and interesting evidence on the efforts to get subsidy from the clergy, and some of it shows that there was opposition: notably A.N., JJ 58, fol. 44 r and v. I am unable to form any clear judgment on the character of the subsidy efforts from the items in Mignon's inventory.

For one thing, by using this approach the king himself was able to take part in the negotiations, and this might well constitute a considerable advantage for the government if resistance were feared. As we know from the complaints of 1315 (and other cases) local officers were regarded as capable of abusing their powers, and some of their abuses had been connected with finance. Any general state of distrust of government officials would make it the more difficult for them to carry through negotiations where consent had to be obtained. Under any circumstances, the representatives of towns would feel freer to argue with and to resist royal agents than to oppose and deny the king. Nor is it merely that reluctant delegates could be overawed by the pomp and majesty of the royal court; moral considerations (of constitutional import) might be on the king's side. This was still a period when subjects thought of the government in personal terms; when they might find it hard to resist the king in person. If the king himself could explain and justify his policy, if he took his subjects (so to speak) into the royal confidence, he might expect results which commissioners would find it harder to obtain.[99] If the king, in 1318, anticipated unusual resistance to a war policy and the attendant taxation,

[99] I suggest that this consideration is implied in the wording of the writs to commissioners who were sent to the towns of central France by letters of January 5. The king takes the trouble to explain why he had not called these towns before him to consult on war policy; this hints that the central towns would argue that they should have been called, that they would feel entitled to the personal treatment enjoyed by the northern towns, that they would not like to have their consent taken for granted. I believe that the same consideration lies behind the phrasing of writs of commission issued by Charles IV in 1326, for Burgundy: cf. *infra*, Appendix.

if he feared dispute on the very principle of aid for war (and not merely difficulties over amounts), then he was well advised to establish the principle through central assemblies as a prelude to local negotiations.[100] This reasoning would be reinforced by the fact that Philip desired to get local negotiations under way months before there could be any official state of war. When a state of war did not exist, when a truce had been established for the purpose of arriving at definite peace, the towns would have the best of opportunity for blocking local negotiations at the very start, on the ground that subsidy was not then necessary, and might not be necessary.[101] Commissioners could not begin by assuming the principle of aid as settled. However, the

[100] The king did not meet the Toulouse assembly, and held no central assemblies for towns of central France. This *could* mean that the king was disappointed by the results obtained at Paris (*supra*, p. 143), but it could also be reconciled with the present argument. If the king got what he wanted at Paris and found that public opinion was better disposed than he had anticipated, he would feel able to forego the trip to Toulouse, and the possible assemblies for the central regions. Note that he makes a point in the letters of October 29, when he announces that he is not coming to Toulouse, of the fact that he is sending members of his "greater and secret council," as though to make up for his own non-appearance.

There is a possibility that the king in any event anticipated less difficulty in raising money from the central towns; i.e., that he may have never seriously planned for an assembly there. This was the region of *villes de bourgeoisie*, without the traditions of strong municipal organization found in north and south. Such towns may have been normally easier to deal with through commissioners.

[101] It is interesting in this connection that as late as June 1319, Philip seems to feel it necessary to emphasize the fact that there *is* a war, in letters calling nobles to military service: A.N., JJ 55, fol. 70, no. 154. The king goes into detail on the fact that the Flemish have raised their standards *in signum guerre*, a thing which the king cannot tolerate. If he needs to make this point clear in June, would we assume that the need for war, or its inevitability, would have been clear during the previous winter?

assembly of Paris forestalled possible delay from that basis of opposition; the towns of the north approved the royal war policy and pledged aid. The local commissioners of subsidy could proceed at once to consideration of the form and amount of the aid promised.[102]

In 1318 the government could not avoid discussion of the principle of aid, as in former years, by presenting an obvious case of military necessity or urgent need. In the period 1302–1304, and (to a lesser extent) in 1314, the king could and did announce a military emergency, declare a general military levy as a matter of right, and send his commissioners to work on that basis. It was a basis (as then used) which did not presume any argument as possible either on the right of the government to demand aid in emergency, or on the existence of the justifying emergency.[103] But no such clear basis existed in January 1319, when war could not come for several months and the government could apparently choose to prevent rather than to plan it.

Viewed in this background, even the minimum results attained at Paris (from the towns of six *bailliages*) had positive value. The Chaumont group promised service of the sort that the government under other circumstances had demanded by declaration of the military emergency. But under the existing circumstances the government could not have called for general personal service and have used that demand as immediate pressure for forcing financial payment; at most the

[102] With limitations to be discussed below in the case of those towns which pledged personal service in an offensive campaign.

[103] Negotiations were still difficult and slow enough; the towns could debate the 'how much' even if the 'whether' was not arguable. On this point, cf. Declareuil, *Histoire du droit français* (Paris, 1925), p. 708.

threat of such service could have been held before the towns.[104] The towns of even the Chaumont group, however, had approved the war in advance, had promised general military service, and could be called on to prepare (by muster) for this service. With this assurance that service (i.e., payment) would have to be rendered in the end, the commissioners had at least some possibility of getting results by negotiation in advance of a state of actual war.

This assurance was the more important because, even under the best of circumstances, the government could not be certain that the principle of general liability for service in response to a summons of the *arrière-ban* would be admitted without dispute. It is true that since 1302 the French monarchy had demanded this service in a form that implied no possible discussion of its right to do so. Furthermore, the charters of 1315 might seem to imply that the royal right was unquestioned, for they failed to deal with this matter at a moment when disputed rights were made an issue.[105]

[104] As was done for purposes not clear in the winter of 1317–18, when both northern and southern towns had received advance warning to prepare for general service in the spring; A.N., JJ 55, fol. 41.

[105] There is also the fact that in 1315, at the very moment when leagues were active and charters were being secured from the government, when the state of public opinion might seem most dangerous to the enforcement of questionable rights, Louis X used the old technique as a means of getting money for a renewed military effort in Flanders! Cf. *H.L.*, X, col. 540 (summons of May 6 to Montpellier); Varin, *Archives administratives de Reims*, II, 164, 169, 171; *Archives historiques du Poitou*, XLIV, 336–337; Giry, *Archives anciennes de St-Quentin* (St. Quentin, 1888), I, 235–236.

But Louis' policy may not be decisive as an argument in the problem here discussed. When he called the *arrière-ban* he had already issued the first series of main charters and had had dealings with the (presumably) most active element of the opposition. I would not maintain that there had been a formal

However difficult it may be to explain the silence of the charters on this issue [106] there is evidence that both before and after 1315 the government met some resistance on the very principle of the liability of townsmen to general military service. The resistance seems to be founded, not on a claim which questions the general

---

process of bargaining; that the charters were a *quid pro quo* for agreement in advance to the *arrière-ban*. However, Louis X had surmounted the crisis, he had assuaged grievances, and he had had an opportunity to explain himself, and to estimate the state of public opinion. Furthermore, there is evidence that the nation was dissatisfied with the inglorious results of the 1314 campaign; public opinion may have been actually favorable toward another effort. Cf. Artonne, p. 71.

[106] Especially in view of the evidence that a main cause of the movement which led to the leagues and charters was exasperation over the subsidy of 1314. This question needs more examination than can be given here, but I should like to suggest one line of consideration. There is no doubt whatever that payment of the subsidy was resisted and that the general movement developed out of this resistance. However, the main ground of objection to payment may have been the fact that collection was being made for subsidy, based on an obligation of military service, *after* the war had ended, *after* it was known that no real military effort had been made, and after the results could be appreciated as representing a failure. In other words, the right of the king to use the *arrière-ban* as a means for getting subsidy may not have been fundamentally involved in the movement of opposition that led to the charters. For clear evidence that Nîmes resisted payment on the basis suggested, cf. Ménard, *Histoire de Nismes*, II, *Preuves*, pp. 18 ff. The first effort made by the government to allay the growing discontent was to stop collection of the tax; by March 1315, it was hinting that money collected before November might be returned (*H.L.*, X, col. 556). Note that in 1313 the royal commissioners of subsidy had been instructed to return the money collected when peace came before the date set for the assembly of troops convoked by the *arrière-ban*; Ménard, II, *Preuves*, p. 11; Funck-Brentano, *Philippe le Bel en Flandre*, pp. 640–641; and *Archives historiques du Poitou*, XLIV, 321. The principle that collections stopped on making of peace, or truce, had been admitted by the government in 1304: cf. *Notices et extraits*, XX (1865), 2, p. 156: *H.L.*, X, cols. 431, 432. My position is in line with Artonne's comments, *Mouvement de 1314*, pp. 18, 19, 26, 29, 43.

liability of subjects to such service, but rather on claims of special privilege for particular towns.[107] This had been the character of the resistance to the first efforts of the monarchy to generalize the obligation of military service, in the reign of Philip III.[108] It is the type of claim specifically made by some towns in 1315: Albi carried its case to Parlement on the ground of "*literas privilegia per que ipsi nituntur ostendere se ad dicte subventionis prestationem non teneri.*" [109] Some townsmen and nobles of Rouergue likewise carried their cases before the king in February 1315.[110] In 1328 there is a very clear case of resistance to the technique of using the *arrière-ban* to get finance, on the part of Lunel; [111] Montpellier [112] denies the obligation of military service but gives money. In 1319 itself, there is the protest of Narbonne, discussed above, against the demand for such service by the royal commissioners at Toulouse.[113]

107 Which would fit with the silence of the charters; they deal with general regional rights and claims, and would not deal with limitations on the obligations to military service unless limitations could be stated in those terms.

108 These cases have been studied by Stephenson in his article "Les aides des villes françaises," *Moyen Age*, XXIV (1922), 318 ff.

109 Letters of Louis X to the seneschal of Carcassonne, January 15, 1315: B.N., Coll. Doat, VIII, fols. 77 ff. It is cited by Artonne, p. 43, but cf. *infra*, n. 114.

110 Text printed in Artonne, pp. 164–165.

111 *H.L.*, X, col. 671.

112 *Ibid.*, cols. 676–680.

113 And there are two other clear cases in 1319. Bourges denied its obligation to render military service outside of Berry, on the basis of privileges (and goes on to decline to give aid on account of lack of means). The text, A.N., J 749, no. 1, is undated: Raynal, *Histoire du Berry* (Bourges, 1845–47), II, 587, publishes the text and dates it 1318, but it is clearly 1319.

An unpublished document (A.N., J 737, no. 42) records an appeal by the town of Pomponne against the demand of the bailiff of Senlis for military

There is no evidence to show in these later cases whether the courts upheld the various claims of exemption.[114] We may doubt that many of these claims were admitted in the end, but it is clear that at least they could still be made and could serve to obstruct and delay negotiations, whatever the outcome. The government might handle the *arrière-ban* as though it gave an unquestioned power to demand general military service, and the towns might not see their way, in 1315, to any clear or general principle of denial; yet there might still be practical reasons (if not clearly constitutional) for the government to get approval, in advance, of the principle of military service.

---

service (i.e., against the obligation of the *arrière-ban!*). The town claims charter freedom from even such military service as involved in a Flemish war. The king orders an investigation; if the town is right, the royal commissioners are not to compel the service (March 14, 1319). This is clear admission by the government that it was by no means so certain of the right to impose the service as the writs imply.

A.N., K 40, no. 21 is an order by the king to suspend efforts to get service or money from the subjects of the Dean and Chapter of Paris until their claims for exemption are settled (March 22, 1319).

[114] Artonne says there is, in the case of Albi in 1315: *op. cit.*, p. 46, "certains . . . avaient plaidé devant le Parlement qu'ils ne devaient payer aucune subvention pour l'ost de 1314 et ils avaient gagné leur cause." Cf. also pp. 43–44, where he says that the discontented elements (southern) won their case completely. But his only evidence (at least cited) is the text from Albi, cited above (*supra*, n. 109), and it does not support Artonne's statement. That text shows that local collectors were ordered to return sums collected since the subvention was rescinded (November), but Albi's claim to exemption from subsidy is referred to the next session for the district of Carcassonne in Parlement. There is, then, no evidence on the outcome of Albi's claim for total exemption and for a return of all subsidy. Nor is there evidence (as far as Artonne cites it, or in my knowledge) of the outcome of the other cases. In 1319, Narbonne seems to have paid money in the end: *H.L.*, IX, 384.

In fact, it is difficult to see what else the government was trying to do in 1314, in its negotiations with the assembly of towns on August 1. As stated earlier, the royal spokesman asked for what seems to amount to a general pledge of 'aid' in the Flemish war: the towns responded to this by a promise of military aid, in most general terms, and "the king thanked them." There seems to be a basic resemblance, in use, between the August assembly of 1314 and the large assemblies of towns in 1318–1319.

There are, it is true, certain differences. In 1314 the assembly, so far as we know, had not been prepared in any way for the business of the occasion, while in 1318 the March assembly [115] had served to warn many towns of the king's plans for a later consultation on Flemish policy. In 1314, the single central assembly may have been constituted on a rather narrow selective basis, that of a summons of *civitates*: in 1318, the king dealt with two large regions by summons to towns on a much broader scale. But above all, in 1314, the king made no formal use of the results obtained at the assembly in the local negotiations for money: [116] in 1319,

[115] *Supra*, p. 112.

[116] On July 25, a week before the recorded date of the assembly, Philip IV issued general orders for the *arrière-ban*: "all kinds of men" are summoned to prepare for armed service and to assemble at Arras on September 8. The letters are dated at Compiègne and addressed to the bailiff of Caen: B.N., ms. fr. 16600, fol. 53. On August 6, *after* the assembly, the king appointed commissioners to enforce the *arrière-ban* and to see that all people render the service demanded. If by any chance some wish to make payment, the commissioners are empowered to commute the service for money (the real purpose, of course, of their commission): *Ord.*, XI, 428–429.

In neither of these texts, nor in the secret instructions given the commissioners (*Ord.*, XI, 429–430, and *Notices et extraits des manuscrits*, XX (1865),

as we see from the writs of January 5, the northern commissioners were to negotiate specifically on the basis of what had been offered at the assembly of Paris in October. These differences are even marked enough to suggest that the purposes for which assemblies were used on these two occasions may not have been basically the same.[117]

But these differences need not force such a conclusion; they could be explained by reference, once again, to the peculiar circumstances of Philip V's effort in 1318. In 1314 the country had only begun to experience the failures of military efforts in Flanders. At the time of the August assembly a state of war actually existed; the king had already convoked the *arrière-ban.* Philip V in 1318 not only had to deal with a disillusioned public opinion, but was proposing to start local negotiations for money in advance of any possible use of the

---

2, p. 214) as to methods of getting money, tactics, etc., does the government make any specific reference to the assembly of August 1, and to the action there taken by the towns.

Artonne, *Le mouvement de 1314*, p. 14, n. 2 suggests that a text published by Petit (*Essai de restitution*, p. 212) belongs with the secret instructions of 1314. But his argument rests on the contention that the demand for secrecy in the text of *Ord.*, XI, 429 is inexplicable in view of the fact that the text concerns the basis (i.e., the definite rate) of the levy, which had been published. But Artonne cites no evidence that they had been published, and there is no such evidence as far as I have discovered. Petit's fragment could fit 1315 as easily as 1314.

[117] And, specifically, they might be argued to show that the government in 1318 aimed at more than it sought in 1314 and more than it got in 1318 — aimed at a definite grant. It prepared for the assemblies in 1318; it planned them so as to include a large number of towns and escape (as far as possible) the difficulties of virtual representation; it was prepared to make specific use of the results obtained at the assembly, and did so as far as these results went.

arrière-ban as an effective means of pressure. Under these circumstances, he might well need to take more preparation, and use more care, to obtain about the same results as given by the towns in August 1314. And under these circumstances, Philip V would have good reason for basing local negotiations on specific reference to the results obtained in the Paris assembly.[118]

The results obtained in 1318 were roughly similar to those secured in August 1314: a pledge of aid for military operations.[119] These results were sought under very different circumstances, and might therefore play differing parts in the respective campaigns to raise money for a Flemish war. In 1314 the government made no definite and formal use of the pledge made by the towns in August.[120] This does not mean that the

[118] Whereas, if Philip IV felt strong enough to declare an *arrière-ban* before the August assembly, there was no reason for him to mention in the writ of August 6 (*supra*, n. 116) that the towns had promised to give what he had already demanded. Furthermore, to make specific mention of such a promise in the writs of August 6 would come dangerously close to formal admission that the king *needed* the consent of the towns for a declaration of the *arrière-ban*. The government was not prepared to make such an admission of principle in 1314 — whatever its practice implied. In 1318, the principle of royal power to declare an *arrière-ban* was still preserved: (1) by the fact that Philip V is getting a promise in advance of a war, for purposes of advance negotiations on finance, and (2) Philip refers to this promise in a way that implies military service as something he could demand of right.

There still remains the question of the secret instructions of 1314. It seems reasonable that Philip IV should have suggested to his commissioners, as a matter of tactics, that the towns be reminded of the pledge of support made by their leaders in the August meeting. Yet this was not done.

[119] Particularized in the case of a number of regions in 1319 as a promise of money payment (in terms of a quota of sergeants), which had greater advantages from the standpoint of negotiations.

[120] Either in the local negotiations for subsidy or (as far as we know) in dealing with the protest on payment of the subsidy in the fall and winter.

meeting was of no service: it suggests rather that we look for its usefulness (and purpose) in the sphere of informal and indirect services. The king was starting a war *and* a drive to raise money for that war. He presented to the leading towns of the country (as to the magnates) his motives, his justification and his needs; they gave him what amounted to a vote of approval on the principle of war and consent to the principle of military aid. The king did not need this action in any formal sense, nor would he use it in a formal way. It could, however, be expected to have its uses in an *informal* way, as background for local negotiations over finance. Leading towns had been taken into the confidence of the king, had been associated in the formality with which the king declared war and justified an *arrière-ban*; they had taken part in the *grant conseil.*[121] These towns might be expected to feel obligated by that association and to serve as examples of loyal support for the local negotiations. It might be hoped that local negotiations on specific subsidy would proceed more smoothly and toward better results than if an *arrière-ban* were simply declared as a means of forcing results.[122]

In 1318 the government could reasonably expect local negotiations for subsidy to be more difficult than

[121] And Philip IV does, in the ordinance for the *arrière-ban* on August 6, refer to the action taken as approved by "*très grant conseil*": *Ord.*, XI, 428, preamble.

[122] We have of course no means of knowing whether local negotiations were in fact aided by these preliminaries. They may not have helped, and this in itself would be a possible further cause for the more elaborate preparations taken by Philip V in 1318, and the specific references, in the writs of commission, to the commitments of the towns at the assembly.

usual, and even than in 1314. It therefore led up to them, as in 1314, by preliminary central negotiations which secured the principle of aid. These negotiations were conducted with as many towns as possible (hence in regional assemblies rather than one central meeting); the commitment of a small number of leading towns might not carry far enough. The commitments on principle made at Paris were emphasized in the local negotiations and became their starting point, because otherwise those negotiations might yield small result until war could be formally opened. The government had more need, and could make more direct use, of results which were superficially the same as in 1314. In both cases the main objective, on this interpretation, was to make local negotiations easier; not to find some other main technique of securing subsidy from towns. In short, these central assemblies were designed as a prelude to the ordinary local campaign for subsidy, and not as a substitute. The further implication is clear: central assemblies were so used because they were thought desirable or necessary [123] for the success of local negotiations.

This reconstruction represents what seems the best interpretation of the government's purpose in using large assemblies of towns, in an effort to get subsidy for war, in 1318–1319.[124] This interpretation, if accepted,

[123] In 1314, "desirable": in 1318, perhaps, "necessary."

[124] It might be well to point out that several of the arguments which were made for the alternative interpretation (*supra*, pp. 142 f.) have already been dealt with in the course of presenting the case here preferred. None of the remaining arguments are in any way decisive. That the king obtained a definite grant from the nobles of Berry does not force the conclusion that the king called all the assemblies of 1318–19, and particularly those of the towns,

has some significance for the history of central representative assemblies in fourteenth-century France.

In the first place, it is suggestive of what may have been a main use of central assemblies in that period: their service as instruments through which the king could get in touch with public opinion in preparation for carrying out difficult national policies. He needed to reach public opinion for several reasons: first, to find out what it was and so to better shape his policy; second, to influence it by the means afforded by such an assembly; third, to commit it, through those present at an assembly, to support, at least in principle, of his policy. The great assemblies of the reign of Philip IV rendered this type of service. In 1302, the dangerous campaign against the papacy was begun by the careful preparation of public opinion in an assembly which

---

in the expectation of getting such results. He might of course try to get as much as possible; in this case he succeeded in getting a maximum. But he was dealing with individual nobles *as individuals*, not as formal representatives of corporate groups, restricted in action by formalities of representative practice. The king might have *hoped* for results of this sort from nobles in regional assemblies and still not have planned these large assemblies primarily because such results might be attained.

The fact that no assembly was held for towns in central France *might* come from the failure of the northern meeting to accomplish useful results — but it could as well come from discovery in the northern assembly that the temper of bourgeois response was better than expected, and that a preliminary assembly might not be necessary.

The preparation for the assemblies of 1318 (made by warning the proctors at the meeting in April) could be an evidence of desire to meet and form an unwilling public opinion rather than of a plan to get specific sums from the next assembly. In any event, this use of the departing proctors in April seems to be opportunism; the king took advantage of the presence of an assembly called for other purposes to introduce the Flemish policy and warn the towns of his plans.

was extraordinarily inclusive of all important elements in the state. In 1308, the morally dubious campaign against the Templars was opened in a way that gave the government, through the assembly at Tours, the maximum chance for effective propaganda.[125] The other early large assemblies are not well known, but could fit well enough into this hypothesis.[126] The meetings of 1317 (March, at Paris and Bourges) are understandable as efforts of Philip V to strengthen his recently acquired title, by using central assemblies as a medium for reaching, testing and forming public opinion.

[125] In both 1302 and 1308, the members of the assembly were asked to commit themselves to the *principle* of the policy at hand. In 1302, the towns and nobles signed prepared letters of protest to the cardinals. In 1308, a chronicler tells us that the king wished to have the "*judicium vel assensum*" of all men of every condition, *lest he be subject to criticism*: *H.F.*, XXI, 650. This could easily be put in terms of the general policy as I suggest it above.

In both cases, the assemblies had further utility: they could be used as a demonstration, in the negotiations with the papacy, of the strength of national support. This feature of usefulness was perhaps the main purpose of the little-known assembly of towns at Lyon-Vienne in 1312: *Etudes Pirenne* (1937), p. 340.

[126] In 1314 (if not 1313) began the use of central assemblies in connection with business for which they were called most often in the next two decades: coinage policy. This was the sort of policy that required delicate handling, and the advantages of preliminary "*conseil*" (with the towns particularly) could obviously carry beyond the practical advice that town experts might give.

There is a very interesting possibility that Louis X planned (and perhaps even met) a number of large assemblies in connection with a proposed war policy in 1316. The only text so far connected with these assemblies is in *H.L.*, X, col. 545 (cf. Artonne's references to it in *Le mouvement de 1314*, p. 98). I hope in a forthcoming study to connect these assemblies with unpublished and undated lists of towns summoned to assemblies, in B.N., ms. fr. 10988, fols. 345–348; Hervieu assigned these lists (without apparent warrant) to 1313. It may be that Louis X in 1316 was planning the sort of use of large assemblies that we find in 1318–19. Cf. *supra*, n. 82.

On the interpretation advanced here, the large assemblies of 1314 and 1318, called in connection with subsidy, were used in accordance with this general principle of service. The king was about to undertake a policy which might be difficult to carry through: that of raising money for war. He had, for carrying through such a policy, ordinary techniques which did not involve central assemblies.[127] In 1314 and 1318, for reasons which we have tried to appreciate, he thought it necessary or desirable to supplement these ordinary techniques by using central assemblies. These gave him what other assemblies had given: the advantage that local opinion had been prepared for the policy at hand and that those elements present had committed themselves on the general principle of that policy.

If all this implies very definitely that central assemblies in France, in this period, had none of the aspects which we ordinarily ascribe to representative assemblies in a later day, that they were not consulted by the king as legislative bodies with definite powers of action, such a conclusion will not surprise students of early representative institutions. There was no reason why representative bodies should not begin to be used, at an early stage, to obtain definite commitments on more than principle (and England could have served here as a contemporary example), but there was no necessity for that sort of development.[128]

[127] Beyond some sort of council of magnates, to approve his decree, as suggested by Beaumanoir's phrase.

[128] These large representative assemblies grew out of, and were enlargements of, the great councils of the earlier feudal monarchy. And while the history of those councils is not clear (and badly needs further study in France) it is fairly certain that they had not acquired any sort of independent con-

However, if such development did not come, the chance for central assemblies to acquire constitutional powers and strength was proportionately delayed. Only the use of assemblies to get definite commitments, particularly in subsidy, would enable assemblies to make definite bargains of constitutional significance. It is a notable feature of French constitutional history that until 1343 (if then) the monarchy never obtained a definite grant from central assemblies of towns. From 1302 on it was making general financial levies, in connection with war, and raising the money by methods which involved getting consent. Not until the Hundred Years War was well under way did the French government actually get a definite subsidy from a central assembly. The cases of 1314 and (especially) of 1318 make this record even more remarkable. Those assemblies seem to be the only cases where large representative bodies were even called in connection with subsidy negotiations.[129] Their use suggests that not only

stitutional role, as a body with powers, by 1300. The principle of main use which I am suggesting here is more or less the principle of the use made of the earlier, more feudal, assemblies.

[129] I know of no possibilities after 1321, as far as there is evidence so far shown in studies of the period. Cf. Coville in Lavisse, *Histoire de France*, IV, 1, p. 11 and *passim*; Picot, *Histoire des Etats Généraux* (2nd ed., Paris, 1888), I; Hervieu, pp. 172 ff. Hervieu argues that an assembly in February 1335 dealt with subsidy, but he has no evidence. The assembly of 1340 (Hervieu, p. 209) seems to be local, as far as the evidence goes. Dognon, *Institutions politiques et administratives . . . de Languedoc*, p. 208 finds no large regional assembly for the south between 1318 and 1346. Cf. above all Viard, "Les ressources extraordinaires," *Revue des questions historiques*, XLIV (1888), 167 ff. This is much more complete than Hervieu and sounder in analysis. I still see no good evidence, however, that the assembly of 1343 "voted" an aid in any form (Viard, pp. 192–3); *H.L.*, X, col. 933 suggests

did the French government obtain no subsidy by definite grants from central assemblies in this period, but *apparently no serious effort was made to do so.* The government managed with local negotiations except when, as in 1314 and especially 1318, central assemblies were judged useful as a preliminary to secure the principle of consent, and to smooth the way for local operations.[130]

---

that this assembly accomplished little more than the meeting of 1318.

It may be that further research will find that some of the large assemblies were used for subsidy in this period. It does not seem likely that *enough* cases will be found to change fundamentally the picture generally held of the period: i.e., that despite three wars (1323, 1326, and 1337) and preparations for a crusade, all involving financial operations, the government used the techniques of local (and sometimes *very* local) negotiations, as far as towns are concerned.

130 There is one seeming exception: the little-known assemblies of 1321. Philip V had a grandiose scheme for general reform of coinage, but it involved buying out all private rights and would be expensive. He brought it before a northern assembly at Paris on July 8 and a southern assembly at Poitiers on June 14. Despite preparations to insure instructed delegations, clergy and towns in these meetings referred back to their constituencies and gave answer later in the year. An assembly of towns for all of France (cf. Varin, *Archives administratives de Rheims*, II, 272; Viard, *Journaux du trésor*, no. 3582, p. 617; and *Speculum*, XIII (July, 1938), p. 300, n. 6) was held at Orléans in October and the answer of Vermandois' towns is recorded. They were asked "what aid the towns would be willing to make to accomplish the matter," and declined to give any. This was probably an attempt to get some sort of direct grant, and the chroniclers show that rumours of a fantastic order were circulating in France as to the hopes of the king (*H.F.*, XXI, 57).

However, this effort to get financial aid was not made in connection with a war and falls outside the regular line of precedents for war subsidy. Furthermore, the government was trying to get finance as a *quid pro quo* for measures which might be expected to have public approval. Therefore, there is not a real parallel between the effort to get money in 1321 and the war subsidies of 1318. I do not see much reason for arguing that if Philip V could conceive of getting a central, definite grant in 1321, he might have had the same ex-

Such are the general implications of that interpretation of the assemblies of 1314 and 1318 which results from the present study, and these implications may seem difficult to accept. We have to account for what may appear a notable lack of initiative on the part of the French monarchy. Local assemblies were used throughout the early fourteenth century for obtaining definite subsidies; central assemblies were used for other purposes; the inconveniences of local negotiations must have been at least as apparent to the French government as they are to us; England was there to furnish examples of the successful centralization of subsidy negotiations in a large assembly. Yet apparently the French monarchy would have made no serious effort to use the centralized rather than the local method of negotiation.[131]

The difficulties thus raised are not a sufficient ground for rejecting, *ipso facto*, the conclusion reached here as to the nature of the central assemblies in 1314 and 1318. They are difficulties, but they are not impossible, by nature, of explanation, and the more complete record of the history of assemblies before 1346 may eventually

pectations in 1318–1319 from the large regional assemblies. The circumstances are wholly different.

[131] The alternative interpretation of the purpose of the assemblies of 1318–1319 would, on the other hand, raise no such problem: it would, rather, aid to solve it. If Philip V called these assemblies to get definite grants and thereby to replace localized negotiations, it is clear that he failed. But we should have at least one clear case of an effort to do what is not (otherwise) seriously attempted for another twenty-five years, and there would be some explanation for that twenty-five year period of delay. The failure of 1318 (plus that of 1321 in a different context, cf. *supra*, n. 130) would have served as an experiment to discourage the government from further attempts at a more centralized mode of negotiation.

clear them up.[132] At any rate, they are problems of the kind which must be faced in getting at the fundamental history of early representative institutions, in France or elsewhere. It may be hoped that this localized study has at least helped to open up the field of such problems.

[132] There would be no point here in doing more than to suggest certain possible lines of solution:

(1) There may prove to be some other case, or cases, than that of 1321 where serious efforts were made to get definite grants by central assemblies. Until the record is more clear, this is always a possibility — though I do not consider it a likely one.

(2) It is at least possible that in such cases as 1314 (though the textual evidence hardly permits it then) or 1318, the government expected no more than it got (i.e., the results were a success) but *experimented* at the time for more definite results and realized that they were not to be had.

(3) It is quite conceivable that there were very obvious difficulties in getting definite commitments from representative bodies even in local negotiations (cf. *supra*, n. 95), that the government knew what they were, and realized that these difficulties would be even greater in negotiations conducted through central assemblies. It is not far-fetched to assume that (*a*) towns preferred to put off commitments as long as possible (*b*) that they distrusted giving such powers (or instructions) to proctors as would be necessary if central assemblies were to make definite commitments and (*c*) that the government would experience all this in local negotiations and would be deterred as a result from making serious efforts to use what seems to us the more efficient method. These very difficulties, plus the disposition of all elements to work in regional groups, hamper the government when it *does* try to get central grants after 1346.

APPENDIX

THE TEXT with which we are concerned [1] falls out of the immediate range of the present study, but there are good reasons for its consideration here. It has a bearing on some of the principles of royal use of assemblies, suggested already in the interpretation of the events of 1318–1319.[2]

The general tenor of the writ is clear and does not demand detailed analysis. Charles IV notifies the nobles and burghers of Burgundy that a state of war exists and that measures of defence must be prepared. He has recently held, at Meaux, a council attended by several prelates, barons and other nobles, to have their aid and council on this business. All of them promised aid from themselves and their subjects. At this point the text comes to the matter of concern for our inquiry. The king says "since, in order to avoid disturbance of your affairs, and expense for you, we did not order you to come to Meaux with those [i.e., the council just mentioned], hoping that you, whom we and our predecessors have always found ready . . . would make such response and aid as the others, in order to make clear to you our intention and the way to proceed in this business we have sent to you our friends and loyal men. . . ." The Burgundians are to hear these commissioners and to grant, do and accomplish what they will ask for the purpose of the war.

Both Hervieu and Langlois, in reporting this text, summarized it to indicate that the king had intended to assemble all elements of the kingdom at a plenary assembly at Meaux.[3]

[1] *Infra*, Texts, p. 198.

[2] The text has, furthermore, some intrinsic importance in the record of early assemblies, since it is one of the very few documents concerning assemblies in the reign of Charles IV.

[3] Hervieu, *Recherches*, p. 177: "cette commission nous apprend que Charles le Bel avait l'intention de convoquer a Meaux des Etats Généraux composés des trois ordres: mais que pour éviter tout déplacement aux mem-

But reference to the text will show (as the translation above indicates) that the king made no statement of what his intention had been, and gives no indication that he had changed his plans. His effort is to explain why he had not called the Burgundians to the meeting which promised subsidy. Obviously, he feels it necessary or desirable to justify that omission; we may legitimately infer that he expects the omission to be raised as a possible obstacle in the way of his commissioners of subsidy. On what grounds could the point have importance?

One possible ground (and it may have been in the minds of Hervieu and Langlois) would be that his subjects expected the principle of subsidy for war to be established in a "plenary assembly." Charles IV obviously assumes that the *principle* (not the amount) of giving subsidy had been settled by the (small) Council of Meaux and that Burgundy will accept that fact. But his care to explain why this meeting had not been plenary might imply that, for the business at hand (establishing the principle of aid) it *should* have been a general and large assembly. In other words, the (constitutional) principle that general assemblies should determine the liability of subjects to a request for subsidy would have crystallized to such an extent by 1326 that the government must justify itself for departing from this procedure.

However, this line of explanation is open to very serious objections. In the first place, it is hard to see how such a principle had had an opportunity to develop to this extent as early as 1326. There is no hint of it in the charters of 1315, when it would have been a useful principle to appeal to if it existed. There had not been, up to 1326, the sort of practice (in approaching levy of subsidy) that would im-

---

bres qu'il voulait appeler à cette assemblée, il préféra leur envoyer des commissaires. . . ."

Langlois in Lavisse, *Histoire de France*, III, 2, p. 281: "Il est dit que le roi a voulu épargner aux personnes et aux députés qu'il avait eu d'abord l'intention d'appeler auprès de lui en assemblée plénière, un déplacement coûteux."

ply the principle.[4] Furthermore, there is no indication in the period after 1326, down to 1343, that any such principle existed: on the contrary, the government used local negotiations (of the type used here for Burgundy) on several occasions which, so far as we know, were not preceded by a large central meeting. An interesting memoir of 1339, drawn up as a minute of possible procedure for levying a subsidy, indicates that the government might use a plenary assembly *or* might employ local assemblies of the type here suggested for Burgundy[5] — but does not imply that the first method is necessary in a constitutional sense.[6]

Finally, there is a much easier and more natural explanation of the king's 'apology' for not calling the Burgundians before him, and one in line with the possibility already noted in the case of the towns of central France in 1319.[7] By this interpretation Charles IV would be trying to get a region (Burgundy) to accept the principle that subsidy was due the king; he wants Burgundy to recognize the principle because it has been agreed to in the small council at Meaux. But Burgundy was not directly (or, at least, not largely) represented in that meeting and the king in person was not honoring the Burgundians with his presence to explain and justify his policy. Therefore, the king justifies himself for not having called them to Meaux and for expecting them, nevertheless, to do as well (*telle et si gracieuse*) as the council of Meaux had done. There would be here an appeal on the basis of example and with it an implied recognition that subjects not approached directly by the king might feel less liable to accept a royal policy than those who had shared in its formula-

[4] The only cases where large central assemblies had operated in connection with war subsidy had been 1314 and 1318; moreover, the latter case was one where a number of large assemblies were held separately.

[5] The text is published by Jusselin in *Bibliothèque de l'Ecole des Chartes*, LXXIII (1912), 229–230. The memoir says, after discussing the first alternative (a plenary assembly), "item se ceste voie ne li plaisoit. . . ."

[6] It may imply that it is more desirable — in the sense that will be suggested below.

[7] *Supra*, p. 133.

tion. On this interpretation, the king recognizes not a constitutional principle but a fact with constitutional implications: that individuals and groups were more liable to accept a policy which they (or their direct representatives) had helped to frame and for which the king *in person* could demand their *concilium et auxilium*; that individuals or groups approached by subordinates of the king would feel less disposed to accept a policy than if they were called into the personal counsel of the ruler.[8]

This 'fact,' if such it be, has ultimate constitutional significance. It helps explain why the king, in matters of grave or difficult policy, had occasionally called plenary councils from 1302 onward — and in 1314 for initiating a subsidy campaign.[9] It has in it the possibility of giving rise to a clear constitutional principle; that important policies (or, specifically, determination of the royal right to demand a subsidy) must be established in a plenary assembly. But that any such principle had crystallized as early as 1326 is more than doubtful; indeed, that it need never crystallize seems to be indicated by the history of the fourteenth and fifteenth centuries.

[8] The document of 1339 (*supra*, n. 5) is extremely significant here. It discusses methods which the king may use in getting consent for subsidy: first a plenary assembly; second "if this is not pleasing to the king" a series of local assemblies *before which the king will appear*; third, local assemblies of the same type visited by commissioners. The third alternative is spoken of as follows "item — ou que le Roy envoiast par les lieus dessus dis certaines personnes pour faire les dictes requestes, *et ceste voie samble la mains convenable*. . . [my italics]."

[9] The problem here touched upon is, from another aspect, the old difficulty, going back to early feudal times, of getting subjects to accept "virtual representation," i.e., to accept the action of a restricted royal council as generally binding. At first a difficulty that mainly affected royal relations with the barons, it could become important in relation to the towns as they acquire organization and strength.

TEXTS

WRITS OF COMMISSION ISSUED FOR *BAILLIAGES* OF NORTHERN FRANCE ON JANUARY 5, 1319

I. MEAUX–PROVINS[1]

PHILIPPUS Dei gratia Francorum et Navarre rex, dilecto magistro Johanni de Paredo, clerico nostro, et ballivo Meldensi, salutem et dilectionem. Exuberantis mansuetudinis plenitudo de fonte regie pietatis egrediens, nunc per pacis tractatus vanos, nunc per treugas, diffusa est multotiens in gratiam recipiendi Flandrenses ad obedienciam ad quam infallibiliter velle venire aut per venie portam sive misericordie januam se dicebant, et ideo sperabatur quod ipsi, pendentibus treugis usque ad instans Pascha solummodo duraturis, apertam eis viam pacis firmarent, et firmatam tenerent, quorum animum ad hoc non perpendimus nec credimus inclinari; existimantes itaque fore cavendi futuris periculis et ne preterito tempori, quod ex dictis eorum et factis variabile comprobatur, futurum respondeat, cum ipsos sub errore rebellionis in eorum cordibus indurato, lapso treugarum tempore, in assueta inobediencie perseverare pertinacia verisimiliter[2] presumamus, cum civibus ac habitatoribus civitatum et villarum plurium regni deliberare voluimus, quibus viis et modis ipsorum Flandrensium protervia,[3]

[1] Archives Nationales, JJ 55, fols. 54v–55r, no. 115. The heading is "Sequntur commissiones illorum qui fuerunt missi ad civitates et villas Regni."

The town of Provins was listed under Troyes (*bailliage*) in the record of towns summoned (*H.F.*, XXIII, 813). In this period the administrative district of Provins did not ordinarily have its own bailiff, but was assigned to the jurisdiction of one or the other of the adjacent *bailliages*; *H.F.*, XXIV, 166 (preface).

[2] Ms., *verissimiliter*.

[3] Ms., *propterva*.

que tam regno quam regnicolis nostris guerrarum dispendia suscitavit irreparabilia, refrenari valeret in casu quo, durantibus dictis treugis, pacem initam non firmarent vel in sua rebellione persisterent obstinati. Et demum procuratoribus seu sindicis predictarum civitatum et villarum pro dicto convenientibus negocio coram nobis et nostro consilio, post tractatus aliquos procuratores seu sindici civitatis Meldensis et ville Pruvinensis, similiter coram nobis in nostri presentia consilii constituti, suo et civitatis ac villarum[4] ipsarum incolarum nomine et pro ipsis, cum summe devotionis affectu quem non immerito commendamus, prestare subsidium certi numeri servientum pro custodiendo fronterias terre Flandrensis seu pro expedicione predicte guerre finaliter consummanda, prout necesse vel magis proficuum videretur, liberaliter obtulerunt. Cuius oblationis devote promptitudinem gratam habentes, et civium ac habitatorum civitatis et villarum[4] ipsarum, sicuti et aliorum subditorum nostrorum quos dicte guerre negocium rem publicam respiciens tangere noscitur, indempnitatibus provideri, et ipsum prosequi negocium ut ad finem actore divino perducatur optatum, cum longe maiori explecto et validiori et aptius ordinato aggressu minorique subditorum incommodo quam lapsis temporibus, desiderabiliter affectantes, mandamus vobis et committimus per presentes, quatinus ad predictas civitatem et villas[4] predicte ballivie vos personaliter conferentes, earum incolas convocetis presentesque vocatos ex parte nostra requiratis ut cum ipsi de aliquo numero servientum promiserint seu offerri fecerint nobis in dicto negocio subvenire, numerum huius, ad stabilitas fronteriarum Flandrensium tam per terram quam per mare dispositas transmittendum et ibidem per anni spatium

[4] There is a serious ambiguity involved in the repeated use of the plural forms of *villa* after initial reference to only the *villa* of Provins. The inconsistency may be due to an error in the initial reference. Comparison with the other writs suggests that the sense of this reference should be to the effect that "delegates of the *civitas* and towns of Meaux and Provins [regional sense]" had made the offer.

The phrasing here could be taken to suggest a series of conferences, the towns of different districts appearing together.

si necesse fuerit tenendum, faciant et exhibeant nobis certum et talem seu tantum qui nobis ipsorum pensatis facultatibus sufficere et honori cedere debeat eorumdem; et quicquid pro dictorum stipendiis servientum iustum et necessarium fuerit exigere et levare, levatumque in aliquo tuto loco apud aliquos viros fideles ipsius ballivie, quos ad hoc de consilio notabiliorum personarum dictorum locorum duxeritis eligendos, et a quibus recuperari possit quod ipsis fuerit liberatum de dicto subsidio vel traditum servientibus ipsis cum tempus advenerit,[5] ministrandum integraliter assignare, in usus alios minime convertendum, studeant et procurent, ad quod celeriter exequendum sollicitudinis et[6] diligencie vestre partes pro nobis interponere festinetis, rebelles si qui fuerint congruis remediis compellendo, sicque scita huius subsidii quantitate super hoc providius ordinare possimus. Et quia gravare non intendimus eos in hoc petendo quod nobis sub quadam benevolencia liberali ut pretangitur obtulerunt, volumus quod peractis premissis per annum ab instanti Paschate[7] numerandum, ad solutionem ulterioris subsidii pro quacumque alia imminente necessitate, occasione predicti Flandrensis negocii, non cogantur, nec sibi per illud quod nobis prestiterint ut est dictum futuris temporibus preiudicium aliquod generetur, super eo litteras vestras patentes quas propter hoc auctoritate regia confirmare promittimus si easdem petierint concedatis eisdem. Si vero alique communitates aut ville predicte ballivie pro dicto negocio coram nobis vocari pretermisse [fuerint],[8] aut procuratores seu sin-

[5] That is, the towns will collect the money and turn it over for safeguard to local committees of responsible men, from whom the royal collectors can get the money when the time comes. The suggestion is that this committee is a safeguard of local interests, in the sense that if the time did *not* come (i.e., if there were no war) the money would not have been paid into the royal treasury in advance. This fits into the argument, developed elsewhere, that the king had to deal very cautiously with the situation because no actual state of war existed.

[6] Ms., *de*. The other writs permit this correction.

[7] Ms., *Pascathe*.

[8] *Fuerint* was written and then cancelled by the scribe. It is found in the parallel phrase in the Caen writ and seems necessary here.

dici earum(dem)[9] presentes predictum vel aliud subsidium pro dicti expeditione negocii non obtulerint, communitates et villas ipsas seu earum incolas requiratis, ex parte nostra, ut ipsi consimile subsidium nobis prestent quod alie ville maiores seu eorum capitanei[10] nobis prestare ut pretangitur obtulerunt; singulares personas [11] in prestatione predicti subsidii sequi viam capitaneorum villarum, seu maioris partis earum aut patrie, negligentes ad hoc faciendum, pen-

[9] The Ms. favors *earum*.

[10] It is difficult to understand the reference here to the captains of the towns. They are spoken of as though they might have been concerned in the offer of *subsidium* (sergeants) made by the *villae maiores*. So far as we know, the captains were not at the Paris assembly. Therefore, the phrase would seem to have reference to the offer of sergeants which the writ assumes will be made by the *villae maiores* to the local commissioners. But even this sense is not clear: it suggests (as do the later references to the captains) that these officers are going to play some part in the local negotiations: that they may serve as mouthpieces of their town in negotiations to determine the form and amount of subsidy. The text allows no more than conjecture: the commissioners presumably had detailed instructions, beyond these formal writs, on such matters.

The suggestion, vague as it may be, is interesting. We should like to know if these captains, instituted in 1317, had been intended to serve such a purpose as is hinted here — or if the king is merely taking advantage of their presence to gain a point in local negotiations. Remarkably little is known of these officers and their actual service. Cf. Lehugeur, *Philippe le Long*, I, 407 and *Philippe le Long . . . le mécanisme du gouvernement* (Paris, 1931), pp. 339 ff.

[11] Some of the details are difficult for me to interpret; here, the instructions with regard to *singulares personae*. It is to be assumed from the context that towns and communities would make corporate settlements on amount, and collect the money themselves. Hence the *singulares personae* might be people who were not affected by the corporate settlements and rates: perhaps individuals who were not members of the municipality for purposes of corporate taxation — like the captains of the towns themselves (officers appointed by the crown) whose assessment is suggested as the standard for these *singulares persone?* It is hard to explain the mention of these "captains" in any other way. On all such technical difficulties as these, we await with impatience the information which can only come from the type of study of the whole question of taxation which has been undertaken by M. Jusselin.

satis ipsarum facultatibus, compellatis, et inobedientes si qui fuerint puniatis remediis oportunis. Damus autem omnibus et singulis fidelibus et subditis nostris presentibus in mandatis quatinus vobis circa hec pareant et intendant. Datum Parisius v[a] die Januarii anno Domini millesimo ccc° xviii°.

II. SENLIS[12]

PHILIPPUS etc., dilecto et fideli magistro Gervasio de Arsiaco, clerico nostro, et ballivo Silvanectensi, salutem et dilectionem. Exuberantis mansuetudinis (*etc. prout in prima usque ad istam clausulam*) et demum procuratoribus seu sindicis predictarum civitatum et villarum pro dicto convenientibus negocio coram nobis et nostro consilio, post tractatus aliquos procuratores seu sindici ville Compendii, suo et ville ipsius nomine cum summe devotionis affectu, quem non immerito commendamus, prestare subsidium certi numeri servientum vel quodcumque[13] aliud nobis placitum[14] iuxta facultates eorum pro expedicione predicte guerre finaliter consummanda,[15] procuratores vero seu sindici civitatis Silvanectensis, suo et incolarum eiusdem civitatis nomine et pro ipsis, venire nobiscum et in prosecutione expeditionis guerre illius personaliter nobis assistere liberaliter obtulerunt, cuiusmodi oblationum promptitudinem gratam habuimus et habemus, sed quia nos, qui dictum guerre negocium, rem publicam respiciens et sic omnes et singulos subditos nostros tangens, ut ad finem actore divino perducatur[16] optatum prosequi, cum minori subditorum ipsorum incommodo et cum longe maiori explecto et validiori ac aptius ordinato

[12] A.N., JJ 55, fol. 56v.

[13] Ms., *quocumque.*

[14] Ms., *placidum.*

[15] Note that apparently Compiègne offered sergeants only for an offensive war, but later in the writ the king refers again to the offer as though it included men for garrison service, as in the case of the Meaux writ. The first reference may, therefore, be a scribal variation, or the second an effort by the government to get more than had been offered, by slipping in the larger phrase.

[16] Ms., *deducatur.*

aggressu quam lapsis temporibus desiderabiliter affectamus, de numero servientum quos villa predicta Compendiensis, et alie ville quas circa hoc credimus eam sequi, pro dicto subsidio nobis prestando disposuerint mittere pro eisdem, reddi voluimus certiores, mandamus vobis et committimus per presentes quatinus ad villam predictam Compendii et alias villas Silvanectensis ballivie, quas eam sequi credimus in hoc casu, vos personaliter conferentes cum incolis seu habitatoribus earumdem tractetis, ut ipsi numerum huius servientum, ad stabilitas fronteriarum Flandrensium, tam per terram quam per mare dispositas, transmittendum et ibidem tenendum per unius anni spatium si necesse fuerit, faciant et exhibeant nobis certum et talem seu tantum qui nobis, ipsorum pensatis facultatibus, sufficere et honori cedere [17] debeat eorumdem; et quicquid pro dictorum stipendiis servientum iustum et necessarium fuerit exigere et levare, levatumque in aliquo tuto loco apud aliquos viros fideles ipsius ballivie, quos ad hoc de consilio notabiliorum personarum dictorum locorum duxeritis eligendos, et a quibus recuperari possit quod ipsis fuerit liberatum de dicto subsidio vel traditum servientibus ipsis, cum tempus advenerit, ministrandum integraliter assignare, in usus alios minime convertendum, studeant et procurent, ad quod celeriter exequendum sollicitudinis et diligentie vestre partes pro nobis interponere festinetis. Civibus et habitatoribus ville Silvanectensis et incolis aliarum villarum, qui eos in nobis oblato predicto subsidio, videlicet veniendi nobiscum et in prosecutione expeditionis finalis guerre predicte nobis personaliter assistendi, sequi voluerint, districtius iniungentes quod ipsi omnes et singuli certis diebus et horis quos successive duxeritis prefigendos conveniant et compareant coram vobis in equis et armis ac alio apparatu in quibus nobis servient, cum tempus accesserit, (ut)[18] sciatur numerus armatorum, tam peditum quam equitum, et videatur etiam conveniens apparatus eorum, iniungentesque ipsis omnibus et singulis quod sic se munitos teneant et paratos,

[17] Ms., *ceddere*.

[18] Missing in the text but necessary to the construction, and found in the parallel writ for Chaumont.

quod ad locum et diem per vos prefigendos eisdem predictum nobiscum negocium aggressuris veniant, submota dilacione qualibet, sufficienter parati, et si aliqui premissa facere non curarent aut minus sufficienter facerent, ipsos ex huius inobediencia vel deffectu puniatis, et nichilominus ad ipsa debite compellatis. Damus autem omnibus et singulis fidelibus et subditis nostris presentibus in mandatis, quatinus ea [19] vobis pareant et intendant. Datum Parisius die v^{a} Januarii, anno Domini m^{o} ccc^{o} xviii^{o}.

III. CAEN [20]

Philippus etc., dilecto et fideli magistro Petro Favuelli, Thesaurio Nivernensi clerico nostro, et ballivo Cadomensi, salutem et dilectionem. Exuberantis mansuetudinis plenitudo de fonte Regie pietatis egrediens, nunc per pacis tractatus vanos, nunc per treugas, diffusa est multociens ingraciam recipiendi Flandrenses ad obedienciam (*etc. prout in aliis usque ad illam partem*). Et demum (*et sequitur*) procuratoribus seu syndicis predictarum civitatum et villarum pro dicto convenientibus negocio coram nobis et consilio nostro, post tractatus aliquos, procuratores seu syndici aliquarum civitatum et villarum ducatus Normannie similiter coram nobis in nostri presencia consilii constituti, suo et civitatum et villarum ipsarum incolarum nomine et pro ipsis, cum summe devotionis affectu, quem non immerito commendamus, prestare subsidium certi numeri servientum pro custodiendo fronterias terre Flandrensis, seu pro expedicione predicte guerre finaliter consummanda, prout necesse vel magis proficuum videretur, liberaliter obtulerunt. Cuius oblationis devote promptitudinem gratam habentes, et civium et habitatorum civitatum et villarum ipsarum, sicuti et aliorum subditorum nostrorum quos dicte guerre negocium, rem publicam respiciens, tangere noscitur, indempnitatibus provideri, et ipsum prosequi negocium ut ad finem actore divino perducatur optatum, cum longe maiori expleto et validiori et aptius ordinato aggressu,

[19] The sense demands that *circa* be supplied before *ea* here.

[20] A.N., JJ 55, fol. 55v, no. 117.

minorique subditorum incommodo quam lapsis temporibus desiderabiliter affectantes, mandamus vobis et committimus per presentes, quatinus ad civitates et villas Cadomensis ballivie vos personaliter conferentes, earum incolas convocetis presentesque vocatos ex parte nostra requiratis up ipsi de aliquo numero servientum ad instar aliarum civitatum et villarum ducatus Normannie in dicto negocio subveniant, et numerum huius, ad stabilitas fronteriarum Flandrensium tam per terram quam per mare dispositas transmittendum, et ibidem per anni spatium si necesse fuerit tenendum, faciant et exhibeant nobis certum et talem seu tantum qui nobis ipsorum pensatis facultatibus sufficere et honori cedere debeat eorumdem. Et quicquid pro dictorum stipendiis servientum iustum et necessarium fuerit exigere et levare, levatumque in aliquo tuto loco, apud aliquos viros fideles ipsius ballivie, quos ad hoc de consilio notabiliorum personarum dictorum locorum duxeritis eligendos, et a quibus recuperari possit quod ipsis fuerit liberatum de dicto subsidio vel traditum servientibus ipsis, cum tempus advenerit, ministrandum integraliter assignare, in usus alios minime convertendum, studeant et procurent, ad quod celeriter exequendum sollicitudinis et diligencie vestre partes pro nobis interponere festinetis, rebelles si qui fuerint, congruis remediis compellendo sicque scita huius subsidii quantitate super hoc providius ordinare possimus. Et quia gravare non intendimus eos in hoc petendo, quod nobis sub quadam benivolencia liberali ut pretangitur obtulerunt, volumus quod peractis premissis, per annum ab instanti Pascate numerandum, ad solutionem ulterioris subsidii pro quacumque alia imminente necessitate, occasione predicti Flandrensis negocii, non cogantur, nec sibi per illud quod nobis prestiterint ut est dictum futuris temporibus preiudicium aliquod generetur, super quo litteras nostras [21] patentes, quas propter hoc auctoritate regia confirmare promittimus si easdem [22] petierint concedatis eisdem. Si vero alique communitates aut ville predicte ballivie pro

[21] Cf. *vestras* in the writ for Meaux, which seems preferable.

[22] Ms., *eadem*.

dicto negocio coram nobis vocari [23] fuerint fuerint (*sic*) pretermisse, aut procuratores seu sindici earundem presentes predictum vel aliud subsidium pro dicti expeditione negocii non obtulerint, communitates et villas ipsas seu earum incolas requiratis, ex parte nostra, ut ipsi consimile subsidium nobis prestent quod alie ville maiores seu earum capitanei nobis prestare ut pretangitur obtulerunt. Singulares personas in prestatione predicti subsidii sequi viam capitaneorum villarum seu partis maioris earum, aut patrie, negligentes ad hoc faciendum, pensatis ipsorum facultatibus, oportunis remediis compellatis, et inobedientes si qui fuerint puniatis. Si vero in dicta ballivia fuerint alique communitates aut ville, que in subsidio huiusmodi de certo servientum numero nobis ut premittitur faciendo sequi viam noluerint aliarum, que nobis predictum certum servientum subsidium ut predicitur promiserunt, et in expedicione ipsius guerre preeligant nobis personaliter assistere, ipsis et ipsarum singulis ac ipsarum habitatoribus districtius iniungatis quod certis diebus et horis, quos successive duxeritis prefigendos, compareant coram vobis in equis et armis et alias convenienter parati, secundum statum et facultates ipsorum, ut per ostensionem huiusmodi sine fictione aliqua sed in propriis equis et armis ac alio apparatu in quibus nobis servient cum tempus accesserit faciendam, sciatur numerus armatorum, tam peditum quam equitum, et videatur etiam conveniens apparatus eorum, iniungatisque ipsorum singulis quod sic se munitos teneant et paratos quod ad locum et diem per vos prefigendos eisdem predictum nobiscum negocium aggressuris veniant, submota dilatione qualibet, sufficienter parati. Et si aliqui premissa facere non curarent aut minus sufficienter facerent, ipsos ex huius inobedientia vel defectu puniatis, et nichilominus eos ad hoc debite compellatis. Damus autem omnibus et singulis *et cetera*. Datum Parisius v^a^ die Januarii, anno Domini m° ccc° xviii°.

[23] Ms., *vobis vocate*, but *nobis vocari*, as in the Meaux writ, seems demanded.

IV. CHAUMONT[24]

PHILIPPUS etc., dilectis Guillelmo Bernardi,[25] Olrico de Noys militi nostris, magistro nundinarum Campanie, et ballivo Calvimontis, salutem et dilectionem. Exuberantis mansuetudinis, etc. (*prout in illa de Meldis et de Pruvino superius scripta usque ad illam partem*): et demum procuratoribus (*post quam sequitur*) seu sindicis predictarum civitatum et villarum pro dicto convenientibus negocio coram nobis et nostro consilio, post tractatus aliquos, procuratores seu sindici nonnullarum villarum ballivie Calvimontis, similiter coram nobis in nostri presencia consilii constituti, suo ac villarum ipsarum incolarum nomine et pro ipsis cum summe devotionis affectu, quem non immerito commendamus, nobiscum venire et in prosequcione expeditionis finalis guerre illius personaliter nobis assistere in equis et armis ac alias sufficienter parati liberaliter obtulerunt. Cuius oblationis devote promptitudinem gratam habentes, et habitatorum villarum ipsarum sicuti et aliorum subditorum nostrorum, quos dicte guerre negocium, rem publicam respiciens, tangere noscitur, indempnitatibus provideri, et ipsum prosequi negocium ut ad finem actore divino perducatur optatum cum longe maiori explecto et validiori et aptius ordinato aggressu minorique subditorum incommodo quam lapsis temporibus desiderabiliter affectantes, nichilominusque volentes de dicto reddi subsidio certiores, videlicet qualiter nobis prosequentibus in persona propria factum guerre valerent assistere, et quam prompte remoto cuiuslibet tarditatis obstaculo nobis guerre negocium aggredientibus subvenirent, mandamus vobis et committimus per presentes quatinus vos aut duo vestrum ad villas predicte ballivie vos celeriter conferentes, preconizari et publice proclamari per villas easdem in locis ipsarum sollempnioribus faciatis, ut omnes et singuli habitatores earum, certis diebus et locis quos successive duxeritis prefigendos, conveniant et compareant coram vobis in equis et

[24] A.N., JJ 55, fol. 55r.

[25] Substituted for *magistro Gervasio Dausy clerico*.

armis et alias convenienter parati secundum statum et facultates ipsorum, ut per ostensionem huius sine fictione aliqua sed in propriis equis et armis et alio apparatu in quibus nobis servient cum tempus accesserit faciendam, sciatur numerus armatorum tam peditum quam equitum, et videatur etiam conveniens apparatus eorum, iniungatisque ipsorum singulis quod sic se munitos teneant et paratos, quod ad locum et diem per vos prefigendos eisdem, predictum nobiscum negocium aggressuris veniant, submota dilatione qualibet, sufficienter parati. Et si aliqui premissa facere non curarent aut minus sufficienter facerent ipsos ex huius inobedientia vel defectu puniatis, et nichilominus eos ad hoc debite compellatis. Damus autem omnibus et singulis fidelibus et subditis nostris presentibus in mandatis quatinus circa ea vobis aut duobus vestrum pareant et intendant. Datum Parisius die v[a] Januarii, anno Domini m[o] ccc[o] xviii[o].

Item alia commissio similis immediate precedenti fuit facta Guillelmo Bernardi,[26] Olrico de Noys, ac ballivo Trecensi pro civitatibus et villis Trecensis ballivie nichil mutato nisi ubi in alia solum loquitur *de villis* in ista loquitur *de civitatibus et villis.*

Item magistro Guillelmo Arrenardi et ballivo Aurelianensi pro dicta ballivia Aurelianensi sicut illis de ballivia Trecensi nichil mutato.

Item (. . . ?) de Arreblaio [27] pro ballivia Senonensi sicut illis de Trecensi ballivia, nichil mutato.

Item Alberti Sancte Genovefe Parisiensis et ballivo Ambianensi pro ballivia Ambianensi sicut illis de Trecensi nichil mutato.

Item similiter Guillelmo Bernardi, Olrico de Noys, et ballivo Vitriaci pro ballivia Vitriaci.

[26] Substituted for *magistro Gervasio* (cancelled).

[27] I read *dtro*, where a name is expected. *Et ballivo Senonensi* has been cancelled (by mistake) and should be included in the phrase.

V. VITRY[28]

PHILIPPUS etc., dilectis Guillelmo Bernardi[29] et Olrico de Noyx militi nostris, magistro nundinarum Campanie, ac ballivo Vitriaci, salutem et dilectionem. Habitatorum villarum ballivie Vitriaci, sicuti et aliorum subditorum nostrorum quos molestum guerre Flandrensis negotium, rem publicam respiciens, non mediocriter tangere noscitur indempnitatibus provideri, prosequique negotium ipsum cum longe maiori explecti cautela quam lapsis temporibus affectantes, mandamus vobis et committimus per presentes quatenus si qui fuerint qui de promissa[30] seu oblata nobis subventione personali, in equis et armis pro dicto negocio faciendo, finare voluerint de numero servientum ad stabilitas fronteriarum Flandrensium vel pro alia dicte guerre expedicione que emergere contingitur, cum eisdem, ne sibi pretacta subventione personali in equis et armis forsitan tediosa vel alias onerosa redditur, de mittendo certum numerum servientum ut predicitur et illud per anni spatium tenendo si necesse fuerit, faciatis financias, consideratis eorum facultatibus et pensatis, idque quod pro stipendiis servientum ipsorum necessarium fuerit sive iustum exigi et levari, levatumque in aliquo tuto loco apud aliquos viros fideles dicte ballivie quos ad hoc de consilio notabiliorum personarum dictorum locorum duxeritis eligendos et a quibus recuperari possit quod ipsis fuerit liberatum de dicto subsidio vel traditum, servientibus ipsis, cum tempus advenerit ministrandum integraliter assignare, in usus alios minime convertendum, sine dilacione qualibet faciatis, ut scita huius subsidii quotitate super hoc providius ordinare possimus. Et quia per huius prestationem subsidii non intendimus ius novum acquirere, nec quod sibi per hoc aliquod preiudicium futuris temporibus generetur, super hoc literas vestras patentes, quas propter hoc auctoritate regia confirmare promittimus si easdem petierint, concedatis eisdem. Damus autem omnibus et singulis fidelibus et subditis nostris pre-

[28] A.N., JJ 55, fol. 57v, separated from the other writs by a blank folio.

[29] Substituted for *Gervasio Dusi clerico* (cancelled).

[30] Ms., *premissa*. In the next line, the Ms. reads *negocia faciendum*.

sentibus in mandatis quatinus circa ea vobis aut duo vestrum pareant et intendant. Datum Parisius v^{a} die Januarii, anno Domini m^{o} ccc^{o} xviii^{o}.

Item eadem Alberti Sancte Genovefe et ballivo Ambianensi.

Item eadem dilectis Guil. Bernardi, Olrico de Noieux militi, et ballivo Calvimontis.

Item eadem predictis Guil. Bernardi, Olrico, ac ballivo Trecensi.

Item eadem magistro Guil. Arrenardi clerico, et ballivo Aurelianensi.

Item eadem Guil. Bernardi[31] et ballivo Senonensi.

[31] Instead of Johannes Arreblaio, in the orders for duplication of the writ for Chaumont (*supra*, p. 189).

THE APPEAL OF NARBONNE, MARCH 14, 1319[32]

ANNO Domini millesimo trecentesimo nono decimo, domino Philippo rege Francie et Navarre regnante, pridie idus Martii. Noverint universi quod existentes in consulatu Burgi Narbone in aula eiusdem consulatus ubi consuetum est consilium ipsius Burgi teneri, pro negociis eiusdem Burgi expediendis, videlicet domini Petrus de Autinhaco, Berengarius Sigarii, Guillelmus de Mossio, Guillelmus Peryerii et Petrus Sicredi, consules Burgi Narbone, et ibidem dicti domini consules, presente eorum maiori consilio et assentiente, tradiderunt et mihi porrexerunt notario infrascripto duas papiri cedulas scriptas, quas per me eundem notarium legi et publicari et romana lingua exponi fecerunt, ibidem appellando, supplicando, protestando et dicendo ut in eisdem cedulis continetur, quarum quidem cedularum tenores sequuntur[33] sub his verbis:

Constituti Petrus de Autinhaco, Berengarius Siguerii, Guillelmus Peyrerii, Guillelmus de Mossio, Petrus Sycredi, consules Burgi Narbone in domo communi consulatus eorumdem, presente eorum maiori consilio et universitatis predicte, dixerunt, quod dominus noster rex Francie et Navarre dudum eisdem consulibus per suas patentes literas suo sigillo regio sigillatas subscripserat sub his verbis:

Philippus Dei gratia Francie et Navarre rex, dilectis et fidelibus nostris consulibus Narbone salutem et dilectionem. Cum super quibusdam bonum statum regni nostri vestramque et aliorum subditorum nostrorum utilitatem et pacem tangentibus ordinare, et super eis vestram et aliarum bonarum[34] villarum partium earumdem deliberationem habere volentes, vos pridem per nostras requisierimus literas ac

[32] B.N., Coll. Doat, LII, fols. 37r–44r. The text is very corrupt. I have made obvious corrections in spelling, and have restored *-ae* forms to the medieval *e*, without indicating these changes in notes. Where the corrections affect possibly the whole form of a word, or the sense of a phrase, I have indicated as much.

[33] Ms., *secuntur*.

[34] Ms., *nostram et aliorum bonorum*.

vobis mandaverimus ut tres vel quatuor idoneas et prudentes ville predicte, plenariam a vobis potestatem habentes concordandi, faciendi et complendi quicquid existeret ordinatum, deputaretis personas, que octava die [ante][35] instans festum Nativitatis Domini apud Tholosam, ubi proponebamus tunc esse, deberent excusatione cessante qualibet interesse, nosque dictam diem ex causa prorogaverimus usque ad quindenam Nativitatis predicte, requirimus vos nihilominus mandantes vobis[36] quatinus dictas personas deputare cum plenaria potestate predicta et in quindena ac loco predictis destinare nullathenus omittatis: nos enim, in casu quo forsan in persona propria non possumus illuc accedere, personas ibidem mittemus de nostro maiori et secretiori consilio idoneas, per quas vestris missis significabimus super premissis et aliis nostrum beneplacitum et intentum. Datum apud Vicenas die dominica ante festum Omnium Sanctorum, anno Domini millesimo trecentesimo decimo octavo.

Quibus literis regiis receptis, supranominati consules ut veri filii et fideles subditi, volentes mandatis regiis obtemperare[37] sicut tenentur et decet, deputarunt certas personas idoneas et prudentes ville predicte, quibus dederunt potestatem concordandi, faciendi et complendi, iuxta dictarum literarum regiarum continentiam et tenorem, que persone sic deputate in quindena ac loco predictis comparuerunt nomine dicte universitatis coram reverendo in

[35] Ms., *post*, so this is a major correction, but necessary in view of the evidence. Otherwise, keeping the *post*, we should have to assume that on July 29, 1318 the king summoned the towns to Toulouse on December 18 (*supra*, p. 114): that on October 29 he postponed this assembly to January 1 (JJ 55, fol. 51, no. 104; *supra*, p. 115); and that on October 29 he issued a second letter referring to his letter *of the same day* and postponing the assembly to January 8! This is impossible, on the face of it. Examination of the text in our Ms. shows that it is (except for *post* and *quindena*) the same text as given in the register (JJ 55, fol. 51). We will therefore assume that either a scribal error was made by the royal clerk in sending the summons, or that Doat's copyist made the error — and the second possibility seems the more likely.

[36] Ms., *nobis*.

[37] Ms., *obtemperate*.

Christo patre domino Raimundo, Dei gratia episcipo Laudunensi, necnon coram potenti et magnifico viro domino Joanne, comite Foresii, ad partes lingue occitane pro regiis negociis per dominum nostrum regem specialiter deputatis,[38] qui domini magistri significarunt personis comparentibus nomine dicte ville, ut dixerunt, regium beneplacitum et intentum, super quibus, de voluntate et beneplacito[39] dictorum dominorum magistrorum, consilium universitatis predicte retinuerunt et diem certam per dictos dominos magistros eisdem personis assignatam nomine dicte ville acceptarunt super responsione facienda de voluntate consilii universitatis predicte, qua die eisdem personis assignata comparuerunt apud Tholosam coram dictis dominis magistris et suam responsionem fecerunt nomine dicte universitatis sub his verbis:

Existentes in presentia reverendi patris in Christo domini Raimundi divina permissione episcopi Laudunensis et magnifici viri domini Joannis, Dei gratia comitis Foresii, ad linguam occitanam pro reformatione patrie auctoritate regia destinatorum, videlicet magistri Guillelmus Hugonis, iurisperitus, Guillelmus de Podaleriis, mercator, procuratores consulum Burgi Narbone et procuratorio nomine eorumdem, dixerunt et responderunt ut sequitur: quod licet gravati sint et depauperati, ipsi et eorum communitas, tam per factum et exactiones contra homines Narbone factas occasione debitorum Iudeorum quam propter financias feudorum et retrofeudorum et propter mutationes monetarum, et propter multa alia gravamina, et etiam quia pannis et lanis non possunt uti ad utilitatem suam et regni emolumentum, ut ab antiquo[40] extitit consuetum, quia etiam pluribus et diversis gravaminibus opprimuntur absque causa rationabili, tam per gardias et custodes portuum domini nostri regis quam regnorum vicinorum, secundum eorum paupertatem parati[41] sunt, ut fideles domini nostri regis suorum antecessorum vestigia fidelitatis sequentes, in suc-

[38] Ms., *deputato*.

[39] Ms., *bleneplacito*.

[40] Ms., *adantico*.

[41] Ms., *parti*.

cursum domini nostri regis contra Flandrenses mittere si et quando[42] guerram dominus noster rex in Flandria habuerit, scilicet consules Burgi ad eorum expensas[43] septuaginta quinque pedites armatos ad tres menses dumtaxat, secundum quod per eos et eorum antecessores de gratia in aliis casibus similibus facere consueverunt; sane prefati domini magistri episcopus et comes, dicta responsione facta, attendentes quod magnificus vir dominus de Suliaco non erat Tholose sed Avinioni, pro negociis domini nostri regis, considerantes quod cum veniret apud Tholosam transitum suum faceret per Narbonam, seu prope Narbonam, voluerunt et ordinaverunt quod, cum dominus de Suliaco predictus, qui ut dicti domini magistri dicebant super premissis melius sciebat regium beneplacitum et intentum,[44] certe persone nomine dicte universitatis coram eodem domino de Suliaco comparerent et eidem dictam responsionèm factam notificarent seu cum eo concordarent, iuxta dicte litere regie continentiam et tenorem. Propter quod predicti consules certas personas deputarunt qui apud Biterris eidem domino de Suliaco nomine dicte universitatis dictam responsionem factam pro dictis dominis magistris notificarunt et fecerunt, que responsio fuit in Narbona coram dicto domino de Suliaco per ipsos consules de voluntate sui consilii ratificata et confirmata; sed dicta responsione non obstante idem dominus de Suliaco precepit et voluit quod certe persone nomine dicte universitatis sequerentur eundem apud Tholosam ratione et occasione premissorum[45] quod fuit dicte universitati multum dampnosum et sumptuosum, salva ipsius reverentia et honore, maxime cum eidem diceretur per consules quod ipse dominus de Suliaco apud Tholosam nomine dicte universitatis aliam non haberet responsionem, quia credebant eam sufficientem, gratam et acceptabilem regie magestati; verumtamen prefati consules, ut fideles domini nostri regis obtemperantes preceptis, dicti domini de Suliaco deputaverunt certas personas

[42] Notice the conditional nature of the grant: cf. *supra*, p. 157, n. 101.

[43] A phrase suggesting a contingent actually found and sent by the town!

[44] The Ms. has a superfluous *quod* here.

[45] Ms., *promissorum*.

que eundem secute fuerunt apud Tholosam, et cum dictus dominus de Suliaco vellet habere eorum responsionem, responsum fuit nomine dicte universitatis Tholose eisdem dominis de Suliaco, episcopo, et comiti memoratis quod dicta universitas[46] stabat et stare volebat in reponsione predicta super his declarata, que responsio facta fuit Tholose die martis preterita ante comestionem, que intitulatur pridie nonas martii. Qua responsione facta prefati domini magistri preceperunt, dixerunt, et ordinaverunt quod omnes incole Narbone, cuiuscumque conditionis existerent, se pararent in equis et in armis secundum statum cuiuslibet, et quod essent et esse deberent personaliter apud Atrabatum in Pascha floria, quod preceptum non fuit iustum seu consonum rationi neque expediens domino nostro regi, salva semper eorum reverentia et honore, potissime[47] cum dicta universitas sit in confinibus regni et prope mare, ita quod esset magnum periculum toti regno et maxime lingue occitane si dicta universitas iuxta preceptum dictorum dominorum sic gentibus spoliaretur et denudaretur, nam posset oriri magnum scandulum et irreparabile, cum inimici fidei Ecclesie Sancte et regni frequentissime discurrere consueverint per maria dicte universitatis vicina, nec nunquam dicta universitas facere tale servicium consuevit, neque prefati domini, salva eorum reverentia et honore, et loquendo semper cum reverentia, dictum preceptum modo predicto facere potuerunt, eorum gratia, honore et reverentia semper salvis, si tenor dicte litere regie diligenter attendatur, cuius fines exacta diligentia sunt servandi, cum super quibusdam bonum statum regni et utilitatem subditorum et pacem tangentibus missi et ordinati sint prefati domini per regiam magestatem; qua re de prefatis comminationibus, ordinationibus, et preceptis modo predicto factis per dictos dominos magistros, fines mandati sui excedendo, in magnum gravamen dampnum non modicum et iacturam regni et universitatis predictorum, prefati consules cum toto eorum maiori consilio se reputant quam plurimum oppressos et aggravatos et verisimiliter ex

[46] Ms., *universitatis*.

[47] Ms., *pontissime*.

aliquibus verbis aliis iamdictis comminatos et fieri mandatos[48] publice per dictos dominos magistros in presentia procuratoris dictorum consulum, suis loco et tempore declarandi et exprimendi si necesse fuerit coram regia magestate, ac ex verisimilibus coniecturis timent per eosdem dominos magistros et quemlibet eorumdem seu per alium, de eorum mandato, in futurum opprimi amplius et gravari; et ideo ex causis predictis et qualibet predictarum supradicti[49] consules de mandato maioris consilii eorumdem et eodem consilio presente volente et ordinante, in his scriptis et infra tempus a iure statutum, ad dominum nostrum regem provocant et appellant, cum super premissis et quolibet premissorum velint scire totaliter beneplacitum domini nostri regis; verum in eo casu ubi non esset licitum a dictis dominis magistris seu eorum altero aliquathenus appellare, per viam supplicationis saltem intendunt et volunt super premissis et quolibet premissorum adire[50] regiam magestatem et de presenti ad eam supplicando recurrunt, ut super his sciant ipsius domini regis omnimodam voluntatem, sub cuius domini regis protectione et tuitione memorati consules eorum consilium et consiliarii eorumdem se ponunt et bona consulatus et propria et singularia cuiuslibet universitatis predicte, epistolas[51] seu literas dimissorias sibi quo supra nomine dari et concedi per dictos dominos magistros semper cum reverentia et cum multiplicata et repetita instantia sepe et sepius postulando, requirentes predictos dominos magistros ut dicte appellationi vel saltem dicte supplicationi, in eo casu in quo non esset licitum ab eis appellare, defferant ob reverentiam regie magestatis, cum de iure in relevamen oppressorum et opprimi timentium dicta remedia fuerint adinventa, et nemini facit iniuriam qui utitur iure suo, protestantes dicti consules quod si presentiam dictorum dominorum magistrorum haberent, dictam appellationem in eorum presentia fecissent, vel in eo casu in quo ab eis non esset licitum appellare predictam sup-

[48] The sense of these words and the phrase immediately following is not very clear.

[49] Ms., *sepedicti.*

[50] Ms., *adhire.*

[51] Ms., *aposlos.*

plicationem eisdem notificarent, et eandem in eorum presentiam fecissent, et infra tempus a iure statutum predicta omnia et singula eisdem cum reverentia intimabunt. Quibus siquidem cedulis lectis et publicatis in dicto loco per me dictum et infrascriptum notarium dicti domini consules, presente et assentiente toto dicto eorum consilio, dixerunt quod ipsi appellabant, supplicabant, protestabant[52] et dicebant in omnibus et per omnia, ut in dictis cedulis continetur, de quibus omnibus et singulis petierunt sibi fieri unum vel plura publica instrumenta per me notarium infrascriptum, volentes et requirentes dicti consules et eorum consilium quod hoc instrumentum fiat, dictetur et ordinetur ad dictam et ordinationem sapientum, licet in iudicio vel extra iudicium, in publicam formam vel aliter, exhibitum fuerit seu productum, substantia tamen in aliquo non mutata. Acta fuerunt hec Narbone in aula predicta dicti consulatus, in presentia et testimonio discretorum virorum magistrorum Guillelmi Hugonis, Guillelmi Audigerii et Joannis Amelii, iurisperitorum, Joannis Fusteri, textoris, Petri Rasoris, furnerii, et Bernardi de Cassio Castello, sartoris, et Berengarii Vesiani, publici Narbone notarii, qui requisitus predicta recepit, vice cuius et mandato, Berengarius Conillaci, clericus Narbone, hec scripsit.

Ego vero Berengarius Vesiani, publicus Narbone notarius memoratus, hic me subscribo et signum meum consuetum appono.

LETTERS TO SUPPORT COMMISSIONERS OF SUBSIDY IN BURGUNDY, OCT. 30, 1326[53]

Charles par la grace de Dieu Roys de France et de Navarre, a nos amez et feaulx les barons et autres nobles et a tous bourgeois et habitans des bonnes villes et lieux du pays et

[52] Ms., *protestabantur*.

[53] B.N., nouv. acq. fr. 7005, fols. 135r–136r. Cf. *supra*, Appendix. I am indebted to Mlle. G. d'Haucourt for assistance in locating the text under its new reference number, and for obtaining photographs of it for my use. It is a copy in the (formerly separate) Brienne collection.

des partyes de Mascon, et de Lyons et du duche de Bourgongne salut et dilection. Vous scavez et est tout notoire comment le roy d'Angleterre meu de sa volente, contre raison en enfraignant la paix qu'il avoit accordee et juree sans ce que en rien y fuissons deffaillant, nous fait plusieurs guerres appertement (?) par li, ses fauteurs alliez et aeidans en diverses parties de nostre royaume par mer et par terre en envahissant et occupant noz villes nos chasteaulx et autres lieux occiant nos gens et nos subgez, boutant les femmes, prenant, emportant et destruiant les biens et domageant le pays en toutes les manieres qu'il onques peust, pourquoy nous qui tiex choses ne povons ne ne devons souffrir, pensans les adrecier a l'aide de Dieu et de nos feaulx amis et bons subges, et resister a la puissance de nos dits ennemis et pourvoir a la seurette et deffension de nostre dict royaume, feismes assembler naguerre a Miaulx plusieurs de nos feaulx prelas barons et autres nobles pour demander advis conseil et aide sur l'accomplisse(ment) de ces besoignes qui tant touchent nous eulx et chacun de nostre royaume; lesquiex oyes les causes dessusdictes, le juste mouvement et le grand desir que nous y avons, conseillerent et distrent qu'il est necessaire que nous eulx et chacun de nos feaulx amis et subgez y entendons sagement et diligeaument et y mettons paine et labeur et façons missions sans espargne, et pour ce chacun de eulx prestement et de grand coeur promist a y faire certaine ayde de soy et de ses hommes et subgiez; et comme pour espargner a vostre travail destourber coustemens et despens n'ordonissons pas que lors vous venissez a Miaux avecques eulx, esperans que vous, lesquiex nous et nos predecesseurs avons tousiours trouvez prez et de bonne volente sans faillir, doyent faire responer et aider telle et si gracieuse comme l'ont promis a faire, nous pour vous monstrer dire et exposer plus plainement nostre entencion et la maniere d'aller avant sur l'accomplissement des choses dessusdictes envoyons vers vous nos amez et feaulx l'evesque de Chartres, nostre cher neveu le Duc de Bourgongne, Gilles Acelin nostre chevalier, lesquiex tous ensemble ou deux diceulx vous vueilliez ouir diligeaument et croire sur ce qu'il vous diront et octroyer faire et accomplir ce qu'il vous requerront de par nous si et en telle maniere que nous, qui grandement nous fions de vous, nous en doyons tenir pour content, et que moyennant vostre bon aide deuement puisse estre pourveu a l'onneur et defension de nostre royaume et seurte de vous et de nos autres subiez et du bien commun; et car nous desirons le bon estat de vostre pais et que se aulcuns de noz officiaulx ou autres vous avoient faict griefs ou autres choses non deues es temps passes, nous pour le relevement de vous et bon adreciment sur ce envoyons esdictes partyes nostre ame et feal clerc l'arcediacre de Paris et Giles Acelin dessusdit a tout plain povoir de reformer le pais corriger punir les torts faitz et les coulpes sur ce, et toutes autres choses faire qu'il verront et congnoistront que soit pour bien de justice sans nulle deport. Donne a Chastiau Thierry le xx jour d'octobre l'an mil trois cens vingt et six. [*et plus bas*-par le Roy en son conseil Tesson-*et sont les lettres scellees en simple queue du parchemin d'un seel de cire jaulne*].